SOCIETY AGAINST ITSELF

SOCIETY AGAINST ITSELF

Political Correctness and Organizational Self-Destruction

Howard S. Schwartz

KARNAC

First published 2010 by
Karnac Books Ltd
118 Finchley Road, London NW3 5HT

British Library Cataloguing in Publication Data

A C.I.P. for this book is available from the British Library

ISBN: 978 1 85575 763 9

Edited, designed and produced by The Studio Publishing Services Ltd
www.publishingservicesuk.co.uk
e-mail: studio@publishingservicesuk.co.uk

www.karnacbooks.com

CONTENTS

ACKNOWLEDGEMENTS

I would like to express my appreciation to a number of people who have helped with the work of this project, through their support and generous criticism. My wife Ann Penner Winston deserves most special thanks. She has not only contributed greatly to this work itself, but has, equally importantly, helped to keep the world off my back and so provided a space within which the work of thinking and writing could take place. She has done all this even though what I was saying sometimes gave her heartburn. Larry Hirschhorn has been my teacher, co-author, colleague, and friend, in all of which ways, I am honoured. Lance Sandelands, Tom Bertonneau, and Leo McNamara also deserve very special thanks for their intellectual support and criticism. Kristo Ivanov read the entire manuscript and made a number of valuable suggestions, for which I am extremely grateful. I am also grateful to Thomas Hoffman, Stanley Gold, Gilles Arnaud, Yiannis Gabriel, Ted Goertzel, David Levine, Howard Stein, Katya Belekoskova, Michael Diamond, Ed Klein, Jim Glass, Jane Shahi, Clara Pracana, Steven Rolfe, and Seth Allcorn.

I would like to thank Phoenix Books for permission to use excerpts from *Burning Down My Master's House: My Life at New York*

Times, by Jason Blair. The late Joan Yalman gave me permission to use material from her case study of Antioch College, which she co-authored with Everett K. Wilson; that deserves a special expression of appreciation. Similarly I appreciate the help afforded to me by Scott Sanders, archivist of Antiochiana. Finally, I would like to thank the School of Business at Oakland University for a Summer Research Fellowship that supported my work on Antioch.

ABOUT THE AUTHOR

Howard S. Schwartz grew up in New York City, where he attended the Bronx High School of Science. His bachelor's degree is in philosophy from Antioch College, and he studied philosophy as a graduate student at the University of Pittsburgh and the University of California, San Diego. His PhD, from Cornell University, is in organizational behaviour. He is a professor of organizational behaviour in the School of Business Administration at Oakland University, and now divides his time between Lake Orion, Michigan and New York City.

Introduction

As Sir Kenneth Clarke (1969) has said:

> Civilisation requires a modicum of prosperity—enough to provide a little leisure. But, far more, it requires confidence—confidence in the society in which one lives, belief in its philosophy, belief in its laws, and confidence in one's own mental powers.

So, when a civilization, like our own, devotes itself to the task of undermining its confidence in itself, this is an act of self-destruction.

There should be no mistaking that this is going on. Examples present themselves nearly every day, and especially within the institutions of culture—our schools, our media, and so on—which are the venues where conveying appreciation for our institutions, if it took place, would have to occur. In this way they have largely undermined the confidence in our goodness that our civilization, like any civilization, needs.

Our children learn that our country is racist, despite the fact that there is no toleration whatsoever for the expression of any kind of racial slur, with new ways of expanding that term being invented every day. They learn that our civilization has a history of slavery, without knowing that this has been true of every civilization, and that what was unique about our own is that we were the first to end it. They learn that America exterminated the Indians, without its being mentioned that this took place through the inadvertent spread of infectious diseases before people even understood how such diseases were spread. They certainly do not learn that our civilization, through science, which has been uniquely its creation, was the first to gain that knowledge. And it has not been conveyed to them that we found ways to use that knowledge to the benefit of all civilizations.

We can say that these cultural institutions represent only a segment of our society, and that other segments remain healthy, but this puts a boundary where one does not belong. The schools are our schools and the media are our media. It is our society's ideas that they are expressing, and not the ideas of someone else.

Such institutions function in society as venues in which we tell ourselves what it means to be ourselves. They do not lack confidence in their expression—a confidence sorely lacking in those segments of our society that maintain whatever belief in the goodness of our civilization that is still to be found. Our cultural institutions regard these segments as retrograde, as unreached yet, and it may well be that they have the power to validate that condescension.

Our society has turned against itself. The question becomes: how did that happen, and why?

Many will say that this has come about through political correctness, and they would be correct, but in doing so they will not really have explained very much. For what is political correctness, and how has it come to have the power to overcome our confidence in ourselves? This is the question to which I have been trying to find an answer for twenty years, and this book represents whatever headway I have made.

I have stuck with what I know, and with the logical development of what I know. This is so in two senses. For one thing, most of the examples I have used are American, because I have greater familiarity with them, but I believe that generalizations to Western society can properly be made. More important is that I have concerned myself with organizations.

The study of irrational processes in organizations is my field, and it is within that framework that the thought presented here unfolds. I have looked at the forces of self-destruction as they have played out in individual organizations, trying to understand their meaning and operation.

But I believe what I am offering has wider application. Civilization, Western or any other, is dependent on organization, and organization depends on civilization. That is not to say the two are the same, but they reflect one another and are coextensive. Showing how they are different is no trivial matter.

So, this book is an exercise in writing large things small. That has its virtues. The study of organizations is manageable in a way that the study of more diffuse social phenomena often is not. One can often be more specific and, in that way, engage facts that enable one to make definite assertions and prove them. In our time, when contending political forces seem to live in entirely different worlds, that capacity for grounding is more than useful.

This is all the more so since the objects of my theoretical work are highly abstract. My claim is that the structure of meaning, the basic framework through which we give sense to our lives, has changed in our society. I try to make sense of this by looking at the origin of meaning, at its emotional roots in the family. There, I see it as a shift in the significance of the mother, the father, the relationship between them, and what all this represents at a number of different levels, with the organizational level being only a particular, though a particularly rich, field of study.

I look at drives towards organizational self-destruction as products of the mind and try to understand the structure of the mental processes that could lead to them. The work does not stand or fall on the basis of commitment to any theoretical principles about the way the world works, but rests on a capacity and willingness to understand one's own mind in a certain way.

The subject matter of this book is irrationality. Trying to understand it as if it makes overt sense is not going to avail us much. But irrationality can be understood rationally, and that is the aim of this book.

This is a work in the phenomenological tradition. The focal point of my understanding is my own mind. I particularly try to comprehend its most irrational elements, as I can best and most honestly understand them. I have found psychoanalytic theory to be of use here, but I use it in the context of my own analysis, and not the other way around. As a result, the work requires no prior commitment to psychoanalytic theory, but only following the arguments I offer on their own terms. These terms are available to anyone willing to honestly consider the data that are available in their own minds.

To Ann, again. And to Robin and Cassie, again. And again in memory of my mother and father, Bob and Hattie Schwartz.

Agave

All ye who dwell in fair fenced Thebes, draw near that ye may see the fierce wild beast that we daughters of Cadmus made our prey, not with the thong-thrown darts of Thessaly, nor yet with snares, but with our fingers fair. Ought men idly to boast and get them armourers' weapons? when we with these our hands have caught this prey and torn the monster limb from limb? Where is my aged sire? let him approach. And where is Pentheus, my son? Let him bring a ladder and raise it against the house to nail up on the gables this lion's head, my booty from the chase.

Cadmus

Follow me, servants to the palace-front, with your sad burden in your arms, ay, follow, with the corpse of Pentheus, which after long weary search I found, as ye see it, torn to pieces amid Cithaeron's glens, and am bringing hither; no two pieces did I find together, as they lay scattered through the trackless wood.

O grief that has no bounds, too cruel for mortal eye! 'tis murder ye have done with your hapless hands. Fair is the victim thou hast offered to the gods, inviting me and my Thebans to the feast. Ah, woe is me first for thy sorrows, then for mine. [Euripides, *The Bacchae*]

CHAPTER ONE

Political correctness and organizational self-destruction*

G iven the importance that organizations give to the idea of diversity, one would think that its virtues would be clear and undeniable. One might be surprised to find that there is no good evidence supporting the value of diversity. Equally peculiar is the fact that the companies who place so much value on diversity do not seem to care whether there is evidence or not.

These were conclusions reached in an article by MIT professor Thomas Kochan and others (2002), which summarized the results of an extensive five-year research project.

At the behest of a non-profit organization called the Business Opportunities for Leadership Diversity (BOLD) Initiative, and with funding from the Alfred P. Sloan Foundation and the Society for Human Research Management, Kochan and his co-authors, a prestigious and well-connected group, undertook their research to provide empirical support for the idea that diversity is a business imperative—support that until that time had been lacking.

---

*Sections of this chapter have been taken from my article "Political correctness and organizational nihilism", first published in 2002, in *Human Relations*, 55(11): 1275–1294.

Their first surprise was that few organizations were interested in participating in the project. Of the more than twenty Fortune 500 companies who were approached, all of whom expressed interest in the research topic, only four agreed to participate, each of which had prior connections with the researchers or the leaders of the BOLD Initiative.

Of more direct importance, though, was the finding that diversity did not have the significant positive effect on organizational outcomes that its prominence on corporate web pages would seem to indicate.

Summing up the findings in an interview for *Workforce Management*, Kochan said,

> The diversity industry is built on sand . . . The business case rhetoric for diversity is simply naïve and overdone. . . . Even when diversity is managed well, the results are still mixed. The best organizations can overcome the negative consequences of diversity, such as higher turnover and greater conflict in the workplace, but that still does not mean that there are positive outcomes. [Hansen, 2003]

As the researchers put it in their scholarly report,

> Despite the variability in industry contexts, specific practices, and performance measures we examined, our quantitative results are strikingly similar. We found that racial and gender diversity do not have the positive effect on performance proposed by those with a more optimistic view of the role diversity can play in organizations—at least not consistently or under all conditions—

Now, they follow this by saying,

> but nor [*sic*] does it necessarily have the negative effect on group processes warned by those with a more pessimistic view. Most analyses yielded no negative effects on team processes at all, but when racial diversity was shown to have a negative effect, it was mitigated by training and development focused initiatives.

Yet, the conclusion that diversity does not generally produce negative effects, or at least negative effects that cannot be mitigated, misses an important point. It is that diversity by itself is an expensive matter; there are costs associated with diversity. At the head of the list one must note that there must be a bureaucracy to organize and administer diversity programmes, and that bureaucracies always have costs. Even the "training and development focused initiatives", which Kochan and his co-workers cite as ways in which organizations mitigate the negative effects diversity can otherwise have, must have costs. He cites estimates of eight billion dollars for training and development alone (Hansen, 2003).

So, what we have here is a matter that is most peculiar. An expensive practice is undertaken by vast numbers of corporations, whom we all know like to think of themselves as concerned with efficiency. One would think that its benefits would be obvious and massive, but, in fact, there is no backing for it.

Yet, in the absence of demonstrable benefits, there is no way of getting around the fact that diversity is a cost without a benefit. It is a loser.

Diversity is a loser?

Having said that, we feel the moral foundations of the universe start to tremble.

Wait!

Let us step back a bit from the logic of the analysis and have a look at ourselves as we are doing it. My wording has been intentionally provocative because I wanted to evoke a reaction. It is this reaction that is of interest to me.

I believe that most people in our society, a number in which I certainly include myself, will respond in a certain way; we respond to a statement like "Diversity is a loser" with a feeling of discomfort and heightened anxiety. We have a feeling of a moral boundary having been violated. The proposition that has been derived has a feeling of moral badness. Perhaps the word "racist" comes to mind, either with regard to the writer of the present piece or the reader, should he or she take the matter seriously. In any case, the feeling of discomfort is palpable, and we find ourselves looking for ways to escape it.

Now, let us note that the process that we are going through, in which we try to evade the conclusion about the costs of diversity, is itself a social process. We are, by now, all familiar with the phenomenon, and associate it with the idea of "political correctness", or PC.

By all accounts, PC began in the university, but, based on my experience with my MBA students, I submit that it has made very powerful inroads in the corporation as well. The point that I want to make is that political correctness is an organizational process, and one that has organizational consequences. It is easy to think of PC as a process that controls what people say, and perhaps we think of it as being limited to that. But reflection tells us that it cannot be so limited.

At the very least, a taboo on saying certain things must affect our behaviour as well, since what we cannot say cannot be used as a justification for an action, or as a reason for it. Hence, if there is any argument to be made for the opposing action, even the most spurious argument, it will carry the day; the opposing action will be adopted. This suggests an answer to the question of how it is that diversity, an expensive programme with no good case to be made that it has positive benefits, has come to be adopted. It suggests the possibility that it has come to be adopted because it is politically incorrect to argue against it.

Moreover, and more importantly, a force as powerful as political correctness must be driven by powerful psychological and social forces whose purposes are served by this taboo on speech. The effects on organizations of these psychological forces must be considered in their own right, and this example suggests that these forces may not be benign.

This chapter is not, despite appearances, about diversity. It is about the forces that underlie political correctness, which I maintain are driving the programmes of diversity; and it is about the effects that such forces may have on organizations, even without regard to those specific programmes.

Diversity may make an organization less efficient than it otherwise might be, but many factors may contribute to an organization's inefficiency. Our judgements here must be relative, and it is by no means certain that diversity stands high on this list.

The problem that concerns me is not with an organization's efficiency, but with its effectiveness. This is not a relative matter, but an absolute one. The question of efficiency refers to the relative cost of doing what an organization does; effectiveness is whether an organization can do what it is intended to do at all. My contention is that the forces of political correctness are antagonistic to the business of an organization, and may undermine its capacity to carry out its function, largely regardless of the relative cost of doing it.

Thus, if we return to our experience of entertaining a politically incorrect thought, we will see that the politically incorrect idea is not simply experienced as one which cannot be said, but one which it is morally bad to speak or think. But what is that bad thought? I suggest that it can be no more than that the organization has requirements that need to be satisfied if the organization is going to survive, and that it has a legitimate right to satisfy these requirements. When this happens, political correctness becomes a moral assault on the right of an organization to exist.

Political correctness and organization

The term "political correctness" was common enough in the left-wing milieu in which I placed myself while I was growing up, but there were significant differences from its usage today.

In its contemporary usage, "political correctness" entered common speech through a *New York Times* article by Richard Bernstein. He defined it this way:

> Central to pc-ness, which has its roots in 1960's radicalism, is the view that Western society has for centuries been dominated by what is often called "the white male power structure" or "Patriarchal hegemony." A related belief is that everybody but white heterosexual males has suffered some form of repression and been denied a cultural voice . . . [1991, Section 4, p. 1]

And:

> more than an earnest expression of belief, "politically correct" has become a sarcastic jibe used by those, conservatives and classical liberals alike, to describe what they see as a growing intolerance, a closing of debate, a pressure to conform to a radical program or risk being accused of a commonly reiterated trio of thought crimes: sexism, racism and homophobia. [Section 4: p. 4]

We can see here that the operative element in PC is the use of emotionally charged accusations: racism, sexism, etc. This is quite different from the original use of the term, which was as a cognitive critique. In its earlier usage, the charge of being politically incorrect, which was never applied to anyone who was not presumed to hold a basic leftist analysis, meant that the accused had misapplied theory; that he was wrong. The contemporary use is an accusation of badness. The first was directed at a thought, the second at a person. Also, the theoretical presuppositions have changed. The issue then was one of class, and the politics were those of class struggle. The basic question was how society should be organized; which class should organize the society in its interest. That is a question that can be engaged through theory, as an abstraction. The politics of PC today are about identity. There is little about the organization of society, and nothing about it is abstract.

These are important differences. PC these days may be said to have a theoretical component, but also an emotional component, which is far in advance of what it had before. The theoretical and the emotional are closely linked, as I will show. However, it is the emotional element of PC that is undoubtedly responsible for its pervasiveness in American society, which is far more extensive than leftist theories, largely advanced through thought, have ever been. In order to understand it, therefore, we need to approach it primarily through the analysis of the emotions it mobilizes, rather than through its theory.

In this chapter, I first explore these emotional processes, showing how they differ from the forces that have created organization. I then show the way in which these destructive elements play out in a syndrome I call *organizational self-destruction*, whose dimensions include the undermining of organizational structure, meaning, motivation, and, ultimately, language itself.

Psychoanalytic theory leads us to focus on the term "patriarch" in Bernstein's definition of political correctness, for psychoanalysis has much to say about the father, and the patriarch can only be that. It enables us to follow that in saying that the castigation of the white male power structure, so common in political correctness, is similarly an attack upon the father.

But what is the meaning of this father, this patriarch? What does he represent that so much of the world is now turned against him? And what will be the consequences, specifically for organizations, of this assault? These are the questions that concern us. In order to answer them, I turn to the psychoanalytic theory of the sex roles, which is based on our early experiences of mother and father. In thinking about this, bear in mind that our ideas of mother and father, which are critical in the way we make sense of the world, are rooted in primitive images, and formed before they could be rationally comprehended. From this, one can see that the feelings associated with these images, and, hence, the basic structures of our understanding, will originate in the primitive, irrational patterns that were in play before we could make conscious sense of the world. Anyone who can accept all this has made room for everything in psychoanalysis that is necessary for our purposes.

Oedipal psychology

Classical psychoanalytic theory is built around the Oedipus complex, which makes the assumption that both the mother and the father participate in the rearing of the child, but have different roles. For this reason, one may say that the classical configuration is *biparental*.

The role of the mother is largely informed by our image of mother as we experience her very early in life. This primordial mother is the world to the infant; her love for the infant is experienced as absolute, unalloyed, and entirely sufficient for every purpose. This love is the fulcrum of the person's basic feeling of being good. This makes her, by far, the most powerful figure in the psyche.

The fantasy (properly speaking, this should be spelled "phantasy", which refers to an underlying, unconscious fantasy. I will refrain from that usage to avoid being excessively didactic) of fusion with this wonderful figure, of returning to a boundaryless closeness with her, lies at the core of whatever we think is desirable. We may think of it as a fantasy of returning to primary narcissism, becoming again the centre of a loving world. Freud calls this idea the *ego ideal* (1914c, 1921c). When we think of our lives as getting somewhere, the ego ideal is where we are thinking of getting. Having an ego ideal, and believing that it is possible for us to attain it, underlies our sense of hope. Without it, happiness is not possible.

According to the traditional psychoanalytic theory of the Oedipus complex, the original rupture of the intimate relationship with the mother is attributed to the father, who has an exclusive relationship with the mother that does not revolve around the child. The child's response to him, as the salience of his relationship with the mother becomes apparent, is murderous rage. He wants to kill the father so that his intimate and exclusive bond with the mother can be reinstated.

In this model, this murderous rage occasions terror at the thought of the father's retaliation, but also a sense of guilt, since the child also loves the father, and this guilt, which involves turning his aggression against himself, provides the basis of civilization (Freud, 1930a). The crucial process here is that the child, having to reconcile itself with the father, introjects the father, internalizes the father's point of view, and undertakes to punish itself for that which the father would have punished. The point, though, is that the father represents external reality. He is serving here as the agent of the society; his point of view represents the basic ideas, values, and rules through which society understands and governs itself. The child then becomes able to form a safe and reliable connection with the father, and with the other members of the society, by learning to govern itself through the same rules that they apply to themselves. This internalization is the basic process of socialization; Freud calls it the formation of the superego. It represents the successful resolution of the Oedipus complex.

Through socialization, over time, we become competent adult members of society, but the infantile images remain, and they retain the power they had when they formed our whole world. These powerful images underlie and inform our ideas of appropriate adult behaviour, especially with regard to the roles of the sexes.

The image of the female continues to be influenced by the early fantasy of the omnipotent, entirely beneficent, loving mother. For both the boy and the girl, the fantasy of fusion with this wonderful figure is at the root of all desire. The problem is that such fusion also represents the loss of individuality, and, hence, the loss of the capacity to defend oneself against any representation of her. She will always be a specific individual in her own right, and, therefore, capable of rejecting us. For this reason, love of the primordial mother also means helplessness in regard to her power

(Chasseguet-Smirgel, 1986). This is so for both sexes, but the boy and the girl must adapt to it differently. The girl's foreboding is mitigated by her capacity to identify with mother, and psychologically appropriate her power. The result is that she can be herself, accepting her emotions, in a way that the boy cannot.

Given his difference from the mother, it falls to the boy to have to "make something of himself" in the world, in a way that will appeal to her. This is a way of developing a countervailing power to the female, which will permit him to get close to her without being helpless before the threat of abandonment. His work in the world, then, is necessary for his independence, in face of the terrible dependence that his emotional life would otherwise represent. He does this by actively embracing the indifferent, external world that he would, otherwise, passively represent by virtue of his difference from mother.

Thus, in the traditional Western psychology of sex roles, the man's life gains its meaning by his engagement with the external world. The father needs external reality so that he can engage it and transform it and, in that way, gain standing with the mother; her respect and appreciation and most importantly, he hopes, her love. He will transform reality in a way that she values, making it amenable and no longer a threat to her, so that she can simply be her loving self, offering the possibility of fusion. In order to do this, the father must learn to deal with external reality on its own terms. He must be able to see himself as an actor among other actors, as others who are not emotionally connected to him see him, as an object rather than as a subject. In the course of this project, he creates what Lacan calls the symbolic order, a register of common meaning, which is available to everyone because it revolves around no one in particular. He is assisted in this by the fact that his emotions are tied up in the woman he loves, in reality or in his dreams, and not ultimately rooted in his working connections. These transactions in the world of indifference require learning a way of seeing himself and the world, which may be called *objective self-consciousness* (Schwartz, 2003).

By internalizing him, the children come to acquire this objective self-consciousness. This enables them to learn what he has learnt about the world through the process of transformation. If they learn what he has to teach, they develop the understanding of an external world, embedded in the symbolic order of shared meaning, which is indifferent to them and operates according to its own terms. They learn to see themselves in these terms, and to draw a realistic boundary around themselves, being able to differentiate between their ideas of themselves and the ideas that others have of them. They learn that most other people will treat them without any special concern, following rules of exchange that apply to everyone and that organize our relations within their mutual indifference; that they cannot have what they want just because they want it, but can only get what they want by doing something that someone else wants them to do.

Yet, the father's bond with the mother conveys the message that the child can gain such a bond, the ego ideal, himself. In a sense, the father is teaching the child a cultural narrative whose theme is the attainment of the ego ideal through the fulfilment of one's social responsibilities. Thus, the child must become like the father, in the sense of becoming a person in the terms of the indifferent, external world. Then he will have earned a place in the world of intimate closeness, as the father appears to have with mother. Thus, the message is that if you do what you are supposed to do, the world will revolve around you with love; you will be able to do what you want and be loved for it. You will be a "success".

This does not need to seem foreign, even to those who think of psychoanalysis as arcane. It does not violate our usual understanding to suppose that children make sense of the difference between family and the wider world by differentiating between "mother" and "father". Mother represents love and intimacy, while father represents the outside world's indifference and its demand for performance. Of course, individual mothers and fathers can and do differ greatly in how they represent these two distinct domains. Some mothers withhold love if their child performs poorly in schools, for example, while some fathers provide the bulk of unconditional emotional support. But the difference in type of relationship remains, and it makes sense to follow psychoanalysis and refer to them as the "maternal function", representing unconditional love, and the "paternal function", representing the indifference of the external world. This is to say that, in symbolizing the world in terms of mother and father, children are not simply describing two important people in their lives, but are expressing a developmental tension embedded in their early experience.

In this sense, Freud is saying that the child navigates this tension by identifying with, idealizing, and internalizing the father. More specifically, the boy wants to become like the father and, thus, take up the role of mastering the outside world, while the girl wants to marry the father or someone like him, thus gaining access, through him, to the resources provided by the outside world. Parents often see these distinctions in children's play when, despite their progressive intentions, boys play with superheroes while girls play "house". This is a very important phase in the child's development. Yet, it is understandable that the child may also have rage against the father and resent him deeply. After all, he represents scarcity, uncomfortable truths ("you are not valued for just being yourself but for what you contribute"), and the struggle that is required for mastery. Yet truths these are, and the pain of subjecting ourselves to them is very much a turning of aggression against the self.

The implication of all this is that the psychologies of love and work are not separate. We identify with the paternal function as a prelude to restoring or recreating the loving world we once had to abandon in the service of maturing. We work in order to regain love, whether we see that in the context of a loving family we create, in the appreciation others show us for the good work we do, or in the rewards we get which signify our importance. We will be able to simply be exactly who we are, doing exactly what we want, and we will be loved for it. In this sense we aim to restore our relationship to mother by taking an indirect route back to her through the world of the father.

We never fully regain that loving world; it is a fantasy of a return to the early state when the world was mother, and she revolved around us with love. But the idea that we can attain it, that we can realize the ego ideal, is what gives our lives meaning. It gives meaning to our lives as a whole and to all the distinct and unlovable things we have to do in the objective world order to gain it, such as our participation in organizations.

However, notice that this programme of socialization is dependent on the premise that the father has earned the mother's love. Remove that presumption and the whole thing falls apart.

Anti-Oedipal psychology

In traditional psychoanalytic theory, it is regarded as a developmental achievement to bring the father into the self. What precedes it is referred to as pre-Oedipal psychology. What marks the development out of pre-Oedipal psychology is that separation from mother is given meaning by the acceptance of the legitimacy of the father. But suppose that separation from the primordial mother were not accepted and, hence, the narcissistic expectation that the world would revolve around us remained our fundamental assumption about life. The thing that seems to the infant to stand in the way of the realization of this fantasy is the father. We already know that the child's response to this is rage and the desire to kill the father. My claim is that the attack upon the patriarch represents a carrying forward of this orientation into adult life.

To see why this is a problem, we must observe that the reason the father is seen as an intrusion into the perfect linkage of mother and child is that he represents the fact that there is a world outside ourselves that does not revolve around us. Reality is what causes the downfall of the idea of living our lives within the perfect circle of mother's goodness. The father did not cause our separation; he is just being scapegoated for it.

I have explored elsewhere the reasons this scapegoating is taking place in our time (Schwartz, 2003). At this point, I will say only that the function of the father was built on engaging reality and keeping it at a distance from the family, so that the mother's love could operate safely within the family. My hypothesis is that he succeeded in that attempt, all too well. For reasons having to do with the remarkable development of organization and technology in the past century, the necessity of directly engaging indifferent reality has been substantially attenuated. As a result, the idea that there is an independent reality that needs to be engaged has lost its conviction.

As a result, the meaning of the father's role has been lost and he has come to be seen, not as a model for our aspirations, but as an invader. He did not earn her love by guaranteeing a space within which her love can operate; but, rather, he took her by force and made her turn her attention away from us, her children. He brought nothing, but took everything. He deprived us of union with her, which would be all that we would need, and to which we are enti-tled. Expelling him, rather than becoming like him, would bring about the ego ideal.

Locating the threat to mother's benevolent omnipotence in the person of the father, then, provides a simple answer to the question of the causes of our distress and at the same time the beginning of a programme for dealing with it. Get rid of him, and life will be perfect.

What we can see from this is that meaning, in this psychology, has a different structure than in Oedipal psychology. In addition to the fantasy of fusion with the mother, the affective core of pre-Oedipal psychology revolves around rage against the father. Meaning is structured here around the rejection of the very devel-opmental achievement that provides the base for socialization in the Oedipal model. Our idea of recreating fusion with the mother means destroying the father, not becoming like him. Giving this structure its due, taking it on its own terms, we would then no longer be able to call it pre-Oedipal at all, in the sense of seeing it as moving toward the traditional resolution of the Oedipal config-uration. I call it *anti-Oedipal*.

Oedipal and anti-Oedipal meaning

In this case, the rage and resentment that the child feels towards the father, and the indifference of the world that he represents, are taken as the touchstone of meaning. In this framework, the world does not have to be a cold, unloving place. We remember our early childhood, when it was not. If it is, it must be somebody's fault. The father, who represents the world's indifference, takes the blame for it. He has unfairly deprived the child of the loving world he origi-nally had with mother. The objective reality he represents is not something we have to learn to survive in, but an affront. The super-ego, which is the internalization of the demands of external reality, becomes an alien presence in our psyche and may come to be seen as internalized oppression. Instead of the idea that you can regain mother's love by becoming like the father, the idea arises that you can reclaim mother's love by getting rid of the father who has stolen it from you. When this is the assumption that is made, the paternal function and its representatives in the outer world, in the form or organizational and social authority are seen as illegitimate.

Rejection of authority can generate a whole world view, and a correspondingly different root for meaning. The father, authority, who has been thought to have earned his love in the objective world, has gained his standing illegitimately. The stories he tells about the external world, and the achievements he wrought within it, are lies.

In the absence of objective reality, there is no basis upon which love can be earned by satisfying the demands that it makes. Differences in the way love has been distributed cannot be based on some having earned more than others, but can only be the result of theft. In fact, his claims about reality have been nothing but lies; part of a strategy to steal the mother's love. The works he claims to have created are only the mechanisms of his crimes.

Specifically, he has stolen that love from those who have not been loved in the past. Those who have not been loved in the past through his oppression are entitled to be defended and loved in compensation. He is to be hated, destroyed, and expelled from the circle of mother's love. When that is accomplished, the world will be restored to its natural condition; a place in which mother's love will prevail, which will make life perfect for us just because we are who we are.

Instead of the cultural narrative that says that if you do what you are supposed to do, you will be loved, the cultural narrative becomes that you are entitled to love, but it has been stolen from you by those hateful, oppressive authorities who now tell you what you are supposed to do. Get rid of him, the narrative continues, take away his power, which is only the power to take from us, and you usher in the power of the mother, which is the power to give to us.

Political correctness

This gives us what we need to understand political correctness. Returning to the definition of PC given above, we can see that it manifests hatred of the father, "called 'the white male power structure' or 'Patriarchal hegemony'". To speak for the father, to buttress his claims about reality, is to participate and collaborate in his theft. Such claims must be vilified and the claim of standing that they support must be attacked as the theft of love of which they are part. The result is "a growing intolerance, a closing of debate, a pressure to conform to a radical programme".

His lies express and define who he is. They have crowded out and usurped the way others would define themselves. In that way, "everybody but white heterosexual males has suffered some form of repression and been denied a cultural voice".

Furthermore, they represent a devaluation and contempt for those who are not heterosexual white males. Hence they are "thought crimes: sexism, racism, and homophobia".

Understood this way, we can see where the emotional power of PC comes from. The image of fusion with the primitive mother is the heart of our desire; but fusion is the dissolution of boundaries. This means that the capacity of those whom we identify with her to love us or hate us is the strongest power that the psyche can contain. This will be especially so, as we have seen, for men. Take away the countervailing power that their work in reality gives them and they are helpless.

The power of the mother can be mobilized and directed by those who identify with her. On that basis, they can offer fusion and create desire; but when that happens, their devaluation and contempt become lethal. The power that comes from this is sufficient to cause a revision of the basic narrative with which people organize and give meaning to their lives.

In this rewritten anti-Oedipal narrative, as we have seen, one's life is given meaning by the offer of fusion with the perfect mother on condition that we reject the father and destroy his works, all of which bring his evil along with them.

These works include organizations.

The meaning of organization in Oedipal and anti-Oedipal psychology

In the simplest possible terms, *organization* refers to the structuring of exchange relationships (Blau, 1964; Homans, 1950). *An organization* refers to a system of exchange relationships that has an identity, in the sense that it is thought of as a specific agent within the overall pattern of exchange relationships. Even on this minimal level, it is easy enough to see that the images of organization that are reflected in Oedipal and anti-Oedipal psychologies are diametrically opposed in a very important way.

Within Oedipal psychology, organization makes sense and organizations make sense. The maternal element is present in the sense of belonging that the organization affords, and in the way that it is seen as a route to the ego ideal. The paternal element is present in the way the organization is understood as being part of the exchange structure of social life. The individual who accepts benefits from the organization will therefore be expected to accept the responsibility of balancing the exchange (Gouldner, 1960).

Focusing on the responsibilities of the exchange process highlights the difference in the way organization is seen from the standpoint of the two psychologies. For a structure of exchange makes objective demands on its participants, demands that need to be fulfilled whether the participants want to fulfil them or not. The paternal element makes it possible for those demands to be legitimized and accepted as obligations. From the standpoint of anti-Oedipal psychology, however, there can be no purpose beyond free expression—no lunches, so to speak, aside from free lunches. It is impossible to make sense of the demands inherent in the exchange framework. They must, therefore, be experienced with rage, and resented as intrusions, violations, and acts of hatred.

These different approaches to organization arise out of fundamentally different structures of meaning and, therefore, different approaches to the nature of reality and to what life holds in store for us. For Oedipal psychology, life is a struggle in which we begin with nothing more than illusion. If we are ever to have anything good in life, we must create it through our efforts. Yet, since it places the ego ideal at the end of a path that we may follow, it offers us hope of its attainment. For anti-Oedipal psychology, we begin with everything that is good, and lose it through no fault of our own. Meaning can be structured only around the narrative of our loss and our hatred of the forces that are seen to have unfairly taken goodness away, and who are seen to have it in our stead. In place of hope it brings us rage, envy, resentment, and *schadenfreude*. And, since that loss is imagined as infinite, these feelings of resentment can never be assuaged or even diminished. They are not passing feelings, but structural elements of the person's orientation towards life.

Within anti-Oedipal psychology, an organization cannot be approached as indifferent, as having some aspects that are congenial to us and some that are not. It cannot seem to be a set of arrangements through which many individuals accomplish their purposes, being, therefore, entirely suited to none of them. Set against the perfect, effortless fulfilment that the primordial mother seemed to offer, the fact that anything is required of us and that anyone else gets anything must be experienced as deprivation: the organization is seen as a locus of oppression, properly the focus of rage, envy, and resentment, and deserving to be destroyed. (In this connection, see the excellent essay by Mark Stein (2000), detailing the ways in which envy attacks social systems.) When these forces are integrated into the organization, they focus the organization on its own destruction. I refer to this process as *organizational self-destruction*. The danger of political correctness, then, is that the dynamics that underlie it incorporate organizational self-destruction into the organization's core processes.

The undermining of organizational structure

As I have said, under Oedipal psychology, an organization may be considered to be a patterning of exchange relationships within a wider patterning. The relationships within the organization, therefore, may be considered to be expressions of what the organization believes it needs to do in order to maintain its status as an agent by satisfying external demands. It expresses these patterns in the form of a structure it imposes upon its participants, beginning with the specifications and standards for of individual jobs. Organizational participants generally grant the legitimacy of the organization's structure as part of their objective self-consciousness, and agree to be bound by it in their activity within the organization (Barnard, 1951). However, the legitimacy of structure is based on Oedipal psychology. Anti-Oedipal psychology, with its denial of external reality, not only cannot make sense of exchange relationships and, hence, organizational structure; it actually comes alive through resistance against it.

Another way of putting this is to follow Weber (1947) in saying that the essence of bureaucracy, or formal organization, is impersonal rules. Anti-Oedipal psychology does not recognize the existence of impersonality. Bringing forward the narcissism of the infant, I experience everything as being about me. If it is not for me, then, it is against me. This means that, within anti-Oedipal psychology, there is an irreducible conflict between the individual and the organization's structure, as specified by impersonal rules.

What we may call anti-Oedipal decay begins when an organization abandons its standards and other elements of organizational structure in order to manifest its love for those who have not, cannot, or will not accept their legitimacy. It is at that point that organizational structure loses its legitimacy and comes to be seen as an instrument of oppression. Making organizational demands, or justifying them in terms of organizational necessity, becomes politically incorrect.

Returning to our discussion of the apotheosis of diversity, we can see that this is where it has its impact. As we saw above, diversity is a cost without a benefit. The idea of its worth, which, by the rules of political correctness, cannot be contradicted, provides the legitimation for affirmative action, in so far as it is undertaken to increase diversity.

Affirmative action illustrates the undermining of standards, since it represents a specification of lower requirements for members of certain designated groups.

Undertaken to provide a marginal advantage to blacks to compensate for their history of discrimination, affirmative action was intended to be temporary and was not intended to translate into numerical quotas, which are recognized as illegal (Edley, 1996). However, it quickly became apparent that a marginal advantage would not be sufficient to make up for strikingly large differences in performance (D'Souza, 1995). The procedures used to implement affirmative action quickly became indistinguishable from a quota system, whether this is acknowledged or not.

There is no sense in saying that racial preferences do not lower standards, since that is exactly what they do, at least with regard to members of the designated groups. We can observe this best in university admissions, where, murky as its workings are, it is at least more transparent than in corporate practice.

There has been no more benefit shown for diversity in university admissions than has been shown in corporate practice. The University of Michigan, in making its case for the use of racial preferences in admissions, asserted that there were educational benefits of diversity (Gurin, 1999). Wood and Sherman (2001) and Lerner and Nagai (2001) have shown their case to be without merit, as a result of the most egregious methodological errors.

For example, the university acknowledged that there are no direct educational benefits from diversity, but claimed, without evidence, that a diverse student body is necessary for various kinds of "diversity exercises" to have effects (Gurin, 1999). These effects, which were quite inconsistent, consisted entirely of self-reported social, attitudinal, and behavioural differences, with no demonstrated connection to grades, test scores, or any other of the usual indices of learning. They could have been entirely accounted for by the supposition that people with certain social attitudes and behaviours would have been more likely to engage in such diversity exercises. Even at that, the magnitudes of the effects were extremely small, and could not have represented significant practical differences.

The Court did not address the validity of the University of Michigan's case, but simply deferred to them. Justice O'Connor said,

> The Court defers to the Law School's educational judgment that diversity is essential to its educational mission. The Court's scrutiny of that interest is no less strict for taking into account complex educational judgments In an area that lies primarily within the university's expertise. See, e.g., Bakke, 438 U.S., at 319, n. 53 (opinion of Powell, J.). Attaining a diverse student body is at the heart of the Law School's proper institutional mission, and its "good faith" is "presumed" absent "a showing to the contrary." [O'Connor, 2003, p. 3]

At any rate, selective universities admit African American and Hispanic applicants with much lower grades and scores on tests like the SAT than white and Asian applicants. There is no dispute about this (e.g., Thernstrom & Thernstrom, 1999).

SAT scores are the best predictor of college grades, for blacks and Hispanics as much as for whites and Asians (Ramist, Lewis, & McCamley-Jenkins, 2001). The SAT has certainly been the subject of criticism, largely for the way it correlates with family income level, a fact that has been taken to indicate a bias (e.g., Lemann, 1999). Now is not the time to go into the technical details of this controversy.

For our purposes, what needs to be understood is that the matters tested in SAT exams are skills such as the capacity to understand difficult books and to engage in complex verbal and mathematical reasoning. These may or may not be related to social class, but they are what college work consists in, and all the more so at selective colleges (Dowling, 1999–2000). By excluding these matters from discourse, the university begins the process of giving up its conception of itself as a place where students read difficult books and engage in complex reasoning. Thus, through political correctness, the organization abandons its capacity to specify the nature of its work, which determines its structure and its place within the exchange framework.

On the other hand, there is not necessarily anything about this that calls for psychoanalytic understanding, and certainly it is not unique. As the supporters of racial preference observe, universities have given preferences to other groups: children of alumni, athletes, and so on. Preferences may be given for bad reasons, but they may still be perfectly rational. Whether specific preferences make sense in terms of the organization's requirements may be an issue, but, to the extent that they can be discussed in a rational way, there is no issue of dangerous unconscious forces. The matter only becomes an issue for psychoanalysis when rational discussion is made impossible. This is exactly the effect of political correctness.

With regard to the issue of affirmative action, the original politically incorrect proposition was that affirmative action was taking place at all, or, at least, that it was taking place in something more than a vague and general way. This was shown in the way that individuals were vilified when they made the facts of affirmative action known. A classic case here was that of Carl Cohen.

Cohen, a distinguished professor of philosophy at the University of Michigan, sought to find out the extent to which racial preferences were being used in admission procedures at the University of Michigan. Receiving a run-around from the University administration, Cohen was forced to turn to the Freedom of Information Act. What he found was that the system of racial preferences was highly systematized and quite extensive. For example, for a white student who did B-minus work in high school (2.8 to 2.99 grade point average), and had test scores in the upper middle range (1100–1190) on the SAT, the chances of being admitted to the University of Michigan were about 11%, according to statistics for the 1994–1995 school year. But, if the student were a member of an "underrepresented minority" and had the same average and test score, the chances of admission were 100% (Cantor, 1996).

For this act, Cohen was subjected to a campaign of vilification for being "racist" that came to a head a year later on the occasion of the university's Residential College, which he had helped to found, announcing that it would name a reading room after him. This provoked a great deal of outrage among some students, most notably through a letter from a black student to the editor of the *Michigan Daily*, which vilified him for being a racist and for creating, through his actions and his defence of them, a hostile climate for students of colour. He urged members of the university to contact members of the administration and protest. The protest was successful. The university backed down on the honour. What needs to be understood in this connection is that Cohen is no right-wing freak. He was a founding member of the Michigan American Civil Liberties Union, and a contributor to *The Nation* magazine, both important institutions on the left side of the political spectrum.

What happened to Cohen is emblematic of political correctness. Valid information is cast out of discourse, not by being refuted through logic or by contrast with other information, but by casting moral aspersions on the individual who divulges the information. In this way, it represents the triumph of subjectivity over objectivity that we know to be characteristic of anti-Oedipal psychology. Yet, that is a general matter. Our present question is a bit more specific. It relates not so much to the issue of political correctness in general, but to the question of how PC is likely to affect organizational functioning. For what we have here is the fact that the information divulged in this case is directly and unequivocally related to expectations of organizational performance. As we have seen, matters tested in SAT exams are the capacities required of college students, and high-school grade point averages are the best measures we have of students' proven ability to accomplish the tasks that a university sets before them in its course of instruction.

But admission standards represent the organization's best judgements about whether an individual will be able to do its work. For the organization to get rid of them would be, in effect, to abandon its capacity to judge whether a product or an individual will suffice to perform the organization's work. And this is the point at which political correctness begins to make inroads into organizational effectiveness and the beginning of the process of anti-Oedipal organizational decay. Through PC, the organization loses the capacity to specify the requirements for its work; indeed, it attacks such specification. Enhancing the approved subjectivity rises to take the place of the organization's work. In the end, the organization, to the extent that it is defined by its work within the overall exchange process, ceases to be viable as an organization. This plays itself out in a number of ways, which we shall consider.

The reformulation of organizational meaning

The nature of meaning requires that issues like the loss of standards must be generalized. One cannot cover a proposition with caveats in one area, and expect it to be taken absolutely in another. Lose standards in one place and you begin a process that culminates in losing them everywhere. This is the reason why PC's potential for destructiveness is as potent as it is. Ultimately, the whole organization, and, beyond that, even the whole *idea of* the organization, the very meaning of the organization, comes under an attack that pushes towards its reformulation. This reformulation is the point to which we now turn.

Political correctness has to generalize. Meaning is structured around the pursuit of a fantasy, and that fantasy is never realized. This means that, in principle, meaning cannot be verified directly. It is, as the postmodernists tell us, always self-referential. That does not mean that how we structure meaning does not matter. It matters very much, because the way we structure meaning has consequences for the way we live our lives and structure our behaviour. In the end, we find that either we are happy with these consequences or we are not. And that matters a great deal. Still, in the interim, our strongest evidence for maintaining our belief in the way our meaning is structured is that others structure their meaning that way. An alternative structure of meaning is a threat to the meaning that our lives have and, inevitably, we move to defuse the threat by extending our sense of meaning over the other, subjecting ourselves to the meaning of the other, or forming a new sense of meaning that encompasses both of them. But such a synthesis requires that the clashing systems of meaning can each be given their due, that they can be spoken, and that their logic and consequences can be considered.

But if one set of meanings is sacrosanct, that means that the contradictory meaning cannot be spoken. The sacrosanct meaning must, therefore, overcome the other without the possibility of synthesis. The point here is that the politically incorrect meaning is regarded, from the standpoint of political correctness, not as a legitimate view that must be weighed in the balance, but as shameful and not possible for the acceptable individual to consider. Another way of looking at this is that, within an organizational setting, there is no way to mark off the areas in which one sort of meaning applies from the areas in which another sort applies except through a distinguishing process that itself has meaning and, therefore, runs the risk of being politically incorrect. If that distinguishing process preserves the negative judgement for the limited group, it will be just as politically incorrect as the judgement made in the limited case.

For example, consider, as a justification for using lowered standards of admission for certain groups of students, the ground that the university is under intense political pressure to do so. This is obviously politically incorrect, because it implies that the university is only admitting those students as a result of coercion and that they would not be thought to belong there under ordinary circumstances. It would violate the cultural voices of the oppressed, who are believed to be entitled to unconditional validation. True or not, it cannot be said, since it implies that the beneficiaries of the preference are a special case marked off by their deficiency. It follows that it is not possible to specify any other way of distinguishing among the requirements for different groups within the organization except by downgrading their importance for everyone.

Once the process of the reformulation of meaning has begun, every process within the organization is brought to go along with it. A major component of this is the undermining of performance appraisal. The redefinition of the organization's demands, promotions, and appraisals as expressions of oppression may be visible in the context of a substantial number of class-action suits brought by black employees against such companies as Texaco and Coca Cola, even when, as was the case with the latter, the company is famous for its support for the black community (Deogun, 1999; Hansen, 2003). Generally, there is no specific evidence adduced and the companies deny the charges of discrimination, but they settle the suits out of court for huge sums, promote members of the aggrieved groups on an accelerated basis, and agree to institute and augment programmes of "diversity training". Texaco and Coca-Cola settled the suits for $176 and $192.5 million respectively (Bloomberg News, 2001). In addition, Coke committed $1 billion for a five-year diversity initiative (Frankel, 2000), and mandated that each of its employees would participate in a four-year diversity training programme.

Of course, in specific cases, these suits may be well founded, but the lack of evidence and the obvious fact that discrimination irrationally deprives an organization of valuable resources and can only be counterproductive leaves another possibility, which is that the image of the company's performance appraisal system as racist is the result of a distortion of perception on the part of the plaintiffs, who have come to see oppression where it is not.

In cases where this is so, the organization is on the route to making itself impossible. If the performance appraisal system was not racist, then what has been stigmatized is performance appraisal itself and, in fact, again, the idea that the organization can make demands on its employees in accordance with the necessities imposed by the exchange process. This point comes into focus with regard to the issue of diversity training, which, after all, represents an attempt to change attitudes. An agreement to emphasize such training must represent the view that there was something systemically wrong with the attitudes that were responsible for the distinctions made in the course of performance appraisal. But if these were simply judgements made on the basis of the organization's necessities, it means that the roots of the crime have been located in the judgements of those necessities themselves. Here, again, the problems this creates cannot be limited to the specific area in which they occur. They must ramify to have the most profound effects on everything that the organization does. Much of this plays out in the context of organizational motivation.

I will turn to that shortly, but, before doing so, there is one other aspect of the reformulation of meaning that requires mention. It is that the meaning of an organization is also the specification of its basic strategy for maintaining a place within the exchange network. It specifies the organization's "distinctive competence", so to speak. But notice that when an organization drops the specification of its work that arises from its distinctive competence, subordinating it to a meaning that is more generic, it itself becomes generic. For example, when the university drops the requirement for understanding difficult texts, under the aegis of celebrating diversity, it begins the process of becoming indistinguishable from every other organization that has abandoned its own distinctive competence to celebrate diversity. So, universities lose their differentiation from high schools, from company training programmes, and from military boot camps, Later on, they all become indistinguishable from glee clubs, road maintenance crews, brothels, and monasteries. When that happens, the differentiation that has defined the exchange network has disappeared. They all become institutions whose purpose it is to celebrate diversity. And this is for its own sake; nothing is exchanged at all.

Undermining of organizational motivation

In the Oedipal organization, the work of the organization is meaningful both under the aspect of exchange and under the aspect of fantasy. As exchange, an organization attempts to maintain a balance between the inducements it offers to employees and the contributions it expects from them in the form of work (March & Simon, 1958). The experience of such a balance is referred to as equity (Adams, 1963). This forms a component of the overall pattern of exchange that gains an organization the support of its environment and permits it to remain a viable entity. Under the aspect of fantasy, such participation is part of the process through which the employee becomes like the father and moves towards the ego ideal of fusion with the mother. But, although this makes sense within Oedipal psychology, it loses its meaning in anti-Oedipal psychology. There, we should recall, fusion with the mother is not something one achieves by becoming like the father, but is something one has been deprived of by the father through his selfishness and oppression.

The very idea that there should be a balance between inducements and contributions loses its meaning and comes to be defined as part of the ideology of oppression. Fusion with the mother can only be imagined through the destruction of the father. However, recall that the father represents reality, and, specifically in this case, the demands that are made upon us as part of the exchange process. He represents, in short, the organization itself. That means that, in anti-Oedipal psychology, what is meaningful is not the work of the organization, but its destruction. This shift in meaning represents a shift in the nature of motivation. This has different effects, depending on whether one is a member of the victim group or the group defined as oppressors.

Within the victim group, the exchange aspect of work disappears and the demands of work come to be experienced as part of the whole pattern of oppressive attacks that have historically marked one's victimhood. This repeats what we saw above concerning the change in meaning; the specific organization, defined by its specific position within the overall exchange network, has disappeared. It has become just another setting for the historical conflict of oppressor and oppressed. The idea of equity loses the component of work contribution and comes to be redefined in terms of the way one sees the historical experience of one's group.

In fact, the individual has disappeared. The subjects of the narratives that give sense to life are groups, not individuals. The individual's life gains meaning only by membership of one of these groups. What is lost is the meaning of anything the individual can do within the context of his specific life, with its specific connections with specific others.

One result of this is that the psychological substrate of work motivation is lost. At best, the work is felt to be meaningless; at worst, it is felt to be an imposition. This, of course, has organizational consequences.

For example, work that is unmotivated and feels meaningless or oppressive is not likely to be done very well. This may be met by decreased valuation by the organization, expressed through a decrease, or a lack of increase, in organizational rewards. For those who have defined themselves in terms of their victimization, these penalties are not likely to be seen as legitimate and will be responded to as further acts of oppression.

Of course, an organization that holds fast to its work demands and performance appraisals will reject such charges. But an organization in the grip of political correctness will be unable to respond in that way and will have to see the judgements it makes as themselves the problem. It will see itself as culpable for the sense of grievance and respond by promoting those who have experienced those demands as oppression and increasing their level of reward.

But though this may have been done to lessen the sense of grievance, it is likely to have the opposite effect. As we have seen, the sense of loss in anti-Oedipal psychology is infinite and irreducible. It cannot be assuaged, but is a structural component of meaning. Advancement only transfers the sense of grievance to a higher level of responsibility. Indeed, the higher demands at that level pose even more of a contrast with the ego ideal, hence increasing feelings of inequity and oppression and multiplying demands for redress. Within anti-Oedipal psychology, these are likely to be met by further reward and promotion, while further decreasing the motivation to work and causing a further deterioration in work quality. All together, this means that decisions of ever increasing importance, affecting ever wider areas of organizational functioning, will deteriorate in quality and may even express antagonism toward the organization. This will lead to further deterioration in the capacity of the organization to formulate its necessities and do its work.

At the same time that the balance of rewards shifts to those defined by their historical victimization, two things happen to those defined as oppressors. In the first place, as the connection between inducements and contributions is attenuated, their contribution becomes relatively devalued. To the extent that they maintain their own sense of the value of their work, this must lead to increased feelings of inequity. Yet, within the politically correct organization, their grievances are going to be redefined as racism or some other form of oppression, and, hence, to provide reason to send them for further abuse in the name of "diversity training" (Lynch, 1997). This cannot help but have a negative effect on their positive valuation of work and, hence, on their motivation.

But while this is taking place, the level of demand placed upon these employees increases, since it becomes their responsibility to make up not only for the work that is not being done by others, but, even more onerous, to make up for the deformations that result from the wreckage of the system of exchange itself. This can only increase their feelings of inequity and decrease their motivation.

This demotivation takes place at the level of exchange. A similar deterioration takes place at the level of fantasy. Specifically, it becomes increasingly difficult to maintain the fantasy of attaining the ego ideal by becoming like father, since the father has been redefined as an oppressor whose moral dereliction makes him unsuitable for connection with the mother. Once sight is lost of the necessities of the organization within the exchange process, those who have been promoted within the organization for doing good work will come to be seen as having stolen their advancement from the oppressed. They will be punished for the work that was previously rewarded. This cannot help but undercut their desire to take on increased responsibility in the organization in the future. Moreover, the hope of promotion was the way that individuals who were identified with the organization dealt with the unpleasant aspects of their jobs (Schwartz, 1990).

For the organization to undermine their possibility of promotion simply removes that way of coping, leaving them feeling stuck with what they hate. In general, as the organization shifts its meaning towards validating the charges of oppression made by those defined as victims, the impact on those defined as oppressors becomes severe.

Indeed, one may easily expect that many will lose the positive basis of their attachment to the company, which provided a large part of the meaning of their lives, having it replaced by bitterness and disillusionment. And these, let us finally note, were the individuals that would have been promoted had performance been the measure. In those terms, they were its best employees.

Altogether, the system of motivation has been turned upside down. Resistance to organizational demands is rewarded and good work is stigmatized. Increasingly, the organization will not be able to maintain the necessary level of employee contribution. In the end, the environment will no longer support the organization and it will fail. At that point, we may say that organizational self-destruction will have succeeded in its aim.

Demotivation in practice: two cases

The Ford Motor Company

According to journalistic accounts, exactly that dynamic came into play not long ago at the Ford Motor Company, as illustrated by several lawsuits filed by employees. In some of these suits, white male employees charged that a forced-choice employee evaluation system was being used, not as a measurement of merit, but as a subterfuge to discharge white male employees, particularly older ones, thereby making room for diversity candidates. An article in the *Detroit News* (Truby, 2001a) tells us:

> The forced ranking system has stoked the already simmering angst over Ford's aggressive push to diversify its workforce and fast-track talented young leaders.

> Ford has set specific goals for hiring and promoting minorities and women and tied executive compensation to meeting those objectives.

> James Fett, a Pinckney lawyer representing Ford employees, said these dictates leave supervisors with little choice but to choose older white males as the C performers.

> "There is a quota system pure and simple," Fett said.

Fett's point needs to be adumbrated. It would be easy enough to dismiss the complaints of those receiving poor appraisals as being self-serving. Fett's point, though, is that the company, by requiring managers to promote women and minorities, has institutionalized their over-valuation in the appraisal system. This necessarily means that, comparatively, white males must be undervalued. When one puts this together with the forced-choice format, the relative undervaluation becomes absolute. This system's objective properties determine that white males will be fired for being white males, and this would be so whether they objected to it or not.

> Fett named [Ford CEO Jacques] Nasser in his suit and plans to use internal Ford documents outlining diversity goals and the CEO's own words against him in court. Nasser, a Lebanese-born Australian, has been candid in saying Ford's workforce lacks diversity. "I do not like the sea of white faces in the audience and Ford Motor Co must ensure that in the future the company reflects the broad spectrum of Ford's customers," Nasser said in an address last year to top executives that was videotaped and subsequently used for diversity training, [Truby, 2001a]

But the suit most directly related to our issue was one filed by a former employee named John H. Kovacs, who claimed that he was the victim of a company-wide practice of reverse discrimination, undertaken to meet aggressive quotas for hiring and promoting women and minorities.

I draw my account of this case from an article in the *Detroit News*, called "Whistleblower takes on Ford; Insider offers documents he says prove the company discriminates to achieve diversity" (Truby, 2001b). The story is that Kovacs, a native Detroiter who began working at Ford in 1992, was an executive in human resources at Ford Credit. Earning about $100,000 a year, he handled the HR duties for three vice-presidents and was privy to the most sensitive personnel matters in his domain. He said that, although he originally idealized the organization, he became disturbed and disillusioned by the blatantly discriminatory hiring and promotion practices that he witnessed there. Indeed, in his view, they affected him directly, since he felt that he had been passed over for promotion to upper management in favour of less qualified minorities and women.

Through his attorney, he wrote a detailed letter to Ford Chairman William Clay Ford, Jr, protesting the company's illegal discrimination against white men. Instead of a response, he was suspended with pay. He subsequently filed suit against Ford and its chief executive, Jacques Nasser.

The issue in dispute was whether Ford practised illegal discrimination by using race and gender to satisfy the diversity goals it had set for itself. Ford denied that it had done so, but Kovacs charged that it had, and he had documents to back up his case. As an HR executive, he had company documents of various sorts that he felt justified his case. These documents included announcements of job openings that specified a preference for minority or female candidates. He also had documents showing that employees chosen as "stretch" candidates, who did not meet the usual criteria but would be given special mentoring, were exclusively women and minorities. But perhaps most damning were minutes of a November meeting at which a top human resources executive announced that no white men could be hired or promoted at management levels for the rest of the year. Speaking of the meeting: "There was a gasp that went up," . . . "The white males in the room just looked at each other."

According to minutes from the meeting on 13 November, included in the suit, Ford Credit undertook the steps to meet diversity goals. "Actions include delaying the hiring, promotion and referral of white males unless there is a good business case to bring them in by year end," the minutes say. "Actions also include the pulling ahead of any promotion, upgrades, referral etc. of non-white" candidates.

What evidently settled the matter for Kovacs was that he was required to inform company executives of the new policy. "It's illegal to do what they were doing and they wanted me to toe the party line," Kovacs said. "There was no way I was going to do that."

The letter he sent to Chairman Ford, and then the suit, were the result.

I have seen the documents filed in this case, and can attest that they have been accurately described here. In fact, Ford's defence did not dispute the authenticity of the documents or otherwise deny the allegations, evidently conceding the validity of Kovacs' claims. Their strategy was not based on refuting his facts, but in attacking him for bringing them to light:

> As Kovacs' accusations and internal documents came to light last week, the automaker went on the offensive—in the courtroom and in the media.

> Ford attorneys, raising questions about Kovacs' credibility, said Kovacs improperly removed personnel records from company premises.

> "They are starting to throw mud at me and take shots at me because I have struck a nerve," Kovacs said. "My name is mud. My career's over in H.R."

Ford's charge that Kovacs "improperly removed" the documents is critically important. It makes no sense to accuse someone of taking documents unless they are real documents. Kovacs went on to say that this was not a matter of his words against Ford's, but rather of Ford's word against Ford's words. Still, Ford evidently believed it could win with this strategy. As Truby (2001b) pointed out, reverse discrimination suits are hard to prove, the Ford legal team is deep and experienced, and the company has the resources to drag the matter out for years: "Ford's best hope is to make it so miserable for this guy that he goes away or he settles," said Ken Kovach, a professor of industrial relations at George Mason University.

From our point of view the important issue is not the legal one, but the motivational one. Here, as Ford tacitly admitted, a policy was in place that denied promotion to some of its employees in order to increase the number of other people in its ranks, even though they were less qualified. In other words, the work that people like Kovacs did was not rewarded as a matter of policy. What made the matter even worse was that their claim to compensation for their work marked them as standing in the way of progress and against the company:

> Ironically, the push for inclusiveness has some feeling forgotten. "We are in the middle of transforming one of the biggest companies in the world," [David] Murphy [Ford's human resources vicepresident] said. "You aren't going to do that by pleasing everybody, by having some kind of consensus. We know we are going to upset some people. Maybe they shouldn't be a part of Ford Motor Co." [Truby, 2000]

Most important, for our purposes, is that they were attacked as being immoral. We can see this from the fact that Ford took on this lawsuit as a moral crusade. Thus:

> During the hearing, Ford attorney Norman Lippitt gave notice that Ford plans to vigorously defend itself against the discrimination claims.

> "I cannot wait to try this case," Lippitt said. "I'm proud to be on the right side of this issue."

Lippitt said Ford is committed to providing minorities and women equal opportunity at all levels of the workforce and won't be dissuaded by disgruntled employees or opportunistic attorneys. [Truby, 2001b]

It is difficult to see how Ford could pursue this strategy of defending itself through the moral condemnation of those who were making a claim to have their work compensated, except by denigrating the moral worth of those individuals and the work upon which they based their claim. Their good work, which previously counted as their claim to reward, came to be the subject of vilification in direct proportion to the value they placed on it by claiming the right to be compensated. The system of motivation had been turned upside down.

What we see in this case is a very good example of our general proposition. Within the politically correct organization, the meaning of exchange is lost. In its place arises a simple morality play, within which those who successfully pursued greater reward through work are seen as having stolen their standing from those who have had less status. Moreover, as can be seen by the fact that their claims are so easily dismissed, this is *all* they are seen as having done. The sense of worth they had obtained through the work that they have done for the organization is now supposed to be a measure of their guilt. Under the circumstances, it is not surprising that the organization would undertake to deal with them in a way that would undermine their motivation.

One place where this demotivation and disengagement would show up would be in the quality of the product, since, as quality gurus like Deming, Juran, and Crosby agree, quality requires engagement and commitment. In fact, the quality of Ford vehicles dropped precipitously. In a "town-hall meeting", held in late September, 2001, Nick Scheele, recently promoted to head of Ford's North American operations, offered a "frank assessment of Ford's vehicle quality:

The company has been plagued by recalls and poor launches in the past year and has seen its quality ratings drop.

"Our quality is not going in the right direction and everybody knows it," he said.

Toyota has increased its quality lead over Ford. And GM and Chrysler have taken significant leads over Ford in key quality areas, Scheele said. [Truby, 2001c]

To be sure, it would be silly to suppose that the demotivation caused by the diversity campaign was the only cause of this. Still, subsequent events indicated that the deterioration in employee engagement had its effect. On 29 October 2001, Chairman Jacques Nasser, the individual most closely associated with Ford's diversity programme, as well as the other elements of its attempted make-over, was fired. The connection with the diversity programme was often explicit:

Nasser was often a divisive figure among Ford employees, who felt that some of his initiatives—such as a forced evaluation system and efforts to promote diversity—created tension in the workplace.

While some Ford employees on Tuesday said Nasser wasn't responsible for all their problems, they said he contributed enough that it was time for him to go. [Donnelly, 2001]

And the effects of the forced-choice system, which, as I have said, was seen, with good reason, as a smokescreen for discrimination against white males, especially older ones, were given special recognition:

The policy spawned a slew of workplace discrimination lawsuits, mostly filed by veteran white male workers, but more importantly devastated morale . . .

Nasser scrapped the policy this summer, but the damage was done.

"He lost the employees," said David Cole, director for the Center for Automotive Research in Ann Arbor. [Truby, 2001d]

Coming under the leadership of William Ford, Jr, the company settled the suits, including Kovacs'. But considerable destruction had already taken place. My argument has been that much of this harm must be attributed to the dynamics underlying political correctness. Nor does the company appear to have backed off from the commitment to diversity that PC has been driving, which may be hypothesized to bear some responsibility for the abysmal condition in which the company now finds itself.

We should be in no doubt about the potential for destruction in what they are doing. We see a bit of this potential actualized in our next case, that of the Cincinnati and Seattle Police Departments.

The Cincinnati and Seattle Police Departments

The most basic visible symbol of the Oedipal dynamic is the law. The law is the direct representation of the minimal necessary demands that members of society make upon one another. It is an expression of what members of the society believe society needs in order to function and in order for exchange to take place reliably within it. As an expression of objective self-consciousness, however, it always runs the risk of being politically incorrect. It is, in fact, because of its obligatory character, the most direct focus of anti-Oedipal consciousness.

Anti-Oedipal consciousness takes the form of an assault on the objective character of law itself. It asserts that there cannot be any such thing as objective law and that law always represents the interests of some groups over others. Sometimes, anti-Oedipal psychology leads to an attempt to reformulate the law in order to enhance the power of those seen as having been oppressed (see, for example, Farber & Sherry, 1997). This view would make it impossible to legitimate power within the society and would make social order impossible. This will be clear to anyone who has followed our argument so far, but its further elaboration will have to wait for another occasion. For the present, what concerns us is the other alternative.

Sometimes the anti-Oedipal drive against the law is directed against those who enforce it: the police. In this case, the police are seen as agents of an oppressive power, not with regard to their specific actions, but as a result of their general function. The very law that they enforce is seen as an agency of oppression. For example, it may be seen as fundamentally racist. Acts of resistance to it are seen as legitimate acts of rebellion and may be engaged in with full moral righteousness. The police who enforce the law are seen and denounced as racist oppressors. When this ascription is taken up by powerful elements within the society, it must have negative effects on the motivation that underlies the job performance of the police. Recent examples of this are visible in the cities of Cincinnati and Seattle.

The case in Cincinnati was catalysed by a riot that took place in 2001. It was of particular interest to me because my wife and I had bought an apartment there in order to visit my daughters at weekends, where they lived with my former wife. I followed the matter closely during the period that it was gaining heavy exposure in the press.

The riot followed the police shooting of a nineteen-year-old black man named Timothy Thomas. Thomas, who was wanted on more than a dozen misdemeanour warrants, ran from police who were looking for him. He surprised one of them, who thought Thomas was reaching for a gun. The policeman shot him in what he thought was self-defence. This police shooting represented the fifteenth killing of a black man by the Cincinnati police within a period of five years. The riot that followed quickly shifted its focus from a protest against police brutality to a generalized attack on white people. This is from an article by John Leo (2001) quoting from the *Cincinnati Enquirer*:

> A mob of black youths . . . dragged a white woman out of her car . . . and into the street, beating her until other neighborhood residents rescued her. Kim Brown, an Avondale resident . . . said members of the mob pulled the woman out of the car and "started busting her up." Another driver assaulted by the mob was Roslyn Jones, an albino black woman, hit by a hail of bricks, one of which struck her in the head. The attack stopped when someone shouted, "She's black!" One witness said: "It was a night of white terror. It turned from a police issue to a black–white issue."

Outside the church, about 200 people surrounded an African drum band, waved African flags, and held signs saying, "It Is Right To Rebel" and "It's Time To Shoot Back" (Sidoti, 2001). In this way, it manifested the view that the police were simply agents of the white race that the rioters thought was oppressing them.

What is particularly significant for our current concern is the way this attitude towards the police was reflected by the news media and the city administration. This is again from columnist John Leo (2001):

> The *New York Times* . . . couldn't even bring itself to use the "r" word. Instead of "riots" it talked of "sporadic protests and vandalism."

This doesn't quite catch the flavor of bricks being heaved through windshields at the heads of motorists, more than a hundred homes and businesses set on fire, or "the bullets whizzing by my head," as one resident put it.

The *Times* mentioned that a police officer was "reported grazed" by a bullet. In fact, a sniper shot him in the stomach, but the bullet deflected harmlessly off his belt buckle up into his clothing. The *Times* said groups of young black men had "alarmed whites." "'Alarmed' is a curious euphemism for what these gangs of rioters were doing to whites," the *Smartertimes* Web site said. Sympathy for the rioters, in fact, poked through much coverage. Call this the "It took violence to bring Cincinnati to its senses" school of reporting. Some of it came close to providing media sanctioning for mob violence. A Page One report in the *Los Angeles Times* said: "(W)hile no one wants to say that the riots were good, there was on Friday an undeniable sense of relief that the mayhem . . . had laid bare Cincinnati's fissures. Now, perhaps, there could be progress." On the Sunday TV show "This Week," an ABC correspondent sounded the same note: "In a week of uncomfortable truths, none has been more uncomfortable than this: It took riots to make people understand how deep are the racial divisions. And it took rioting for people to feel the urgency required to close those divides." Listen up, Cincinnati: Riots are good for you. We here at the network think they are a growth opportunity

And this is from Heather MacDonald (2003):

Local leaders scrambled to contain the public-relations fiasco and to show their concern for black anger. The City Council hurriedly voted to submit a pending racial-profiling lawsuit to costly "mediation," rather than contest it, even though none of the suit's allegations had been shown to be credible. Mayor Luken invited in the Justice Department to investigate the police division, which could result in federal oversight of the kind that busts municipal budgets. But the city's main riot response was to form Community Action Now (CAN), a three-man panel dedicated to racial reconciliation through, as its members and promotional materials insist, action, action, and more action. Its three co-chairs are Ross Love, an ex-Procter & Gamble vice president who now heads a black radio empire; Tom Cody, an executive vice president of Federated Department Stores; and the Reverend Damon Lynch, the activist who calls the police "dogs." [p. 66]

Of course, all of this contrition would have been in order if the police had, in fact, been engaging in the programme of extermination of innocent blacks that their critics charged. But the simple truth is that they were not. With regard to the killings of the fifteen black men, a review of the cases by the *Cincinnati Enquirer* found that five were actually shooting or pointing a gun at the police at the time of their killing, and four were attacking the police with a variety of other weapons, including a nail-studded two-by-four and a car. Another two had guns and were threatening to use them. In one case, the man evidently died of a cocaine-induced condition while in custody, not as a result of police activity. In another case, the circumstances were unclear, but the officer was exonerated in a US Department of Justice investigation. In only one case, that of a suspect who suffocated after having been sprayed with a chemical irritant, could a serious charge of dereliction be made, and in that case two of the officers involved were indicted (Klepal & Andrews, 2001). Nor does it appear that the number of police killings of blacks was extraordinary. As Leo (2001) noted, the Cincinnati police force was far from being the nation's most trigger-happy. He cited, as evidence, a 1998 story in the *Washington Post* reporting that Washington's police department had killed fifty-seven people in the previous five years. Another story, this time in the *Detroit Free Press*, reported in 2002 that Detroit police had been killing nearly ten civilians per year. And these figures were despite the fact that both of the police forces were largely black.

Actually, again according to MacDonald, "with a death toll of three officers over the last four years, a Cincinnati cop is 27 times more likely to die at the hands of a black man than a black man is to die at the hands of the Cincinnati police".

Under the circumstances, it appears that the issue arose in Cincinnati only because some wanted to make an issue of the tension that was already there. And, in accordance with our model, it appears that the heart of the issue, the main crime for which the police were being held responsible, was just that they were being police. Actually, as Leo notes, an issue that has caught no one's attention is that the Cincinnati police force is about a quarter black, and so were about a quarter of those who had been involved in these killings. They must justifiably have felt the vilification they received from the city administration and the media as the consequence of doing their jobs. For them, in the pattern that we have described, the world had been turned upside down. Rather than being rewarded for doing their jobs, they were punished. Instead of being seen as the good guys for doing their work, they are seen as the bad guys.

We would expect consequences from this in terms of their work motivation and these consequences were not long in coming. Police drew back from the job of law enforcement in Cincinnati. David Horowitz (2001) put the matter this way:

> Consider the perspective of an underrepresented party in these events: the law enforcement community in Cincinnati. This community was in the habit of reading Miranda rights to every predator it arrested however calculating and vile his criminal misdeeds. But now it saw itself presumed guilty in front of the entire nation, before evidence of any crime had even been presented. This community had witnessed a swifter indictment lodged against one of its own than that of many of the felons it had pursued. Overnight, and without probable cause, it had become the target of a national lynch mob seeking "justice" from a policeman for the crime of performing his protective duty. In advance of any trial or presentation of the facts, this community could not fail to notice that it had been put in the criminal dock and had no defenders in the national press or even among city officials who were pledged to uphold the law and support the public good.

And he quotes a newsletter to members of the Cincinnati Fraternal Order of Police from its president, Kenneth Fangman:

> If you want to make 20 traffic stops a shift and chase every dope dealer you see, you go right ahead. Just remember that if something goes wrong, or you make the slightest mistake in that split second, it could result in having your worst nightmare come true for you and your family, and City Hall will sell you out.

After a while, this matter even caught the attention of the *New York Times:*

> Three months after this city was traumatized by street clashes and vandalism, the police have retreated from "proactive" patrols in black neighborhoods, saying they fear fresh charges of racism.

Arrests have dropped 50 percent since mid-April, he said, insisting that it was not a job action and that his officers wanted to be pro-active.

But, Mr. Fangman said, they were "shellshocked" by a lack of polit-ical support and a rising tide of investigations and complaints.

The police chief, Tom Streicher, has expressed sympathy for his officers, describing an "air of permissiveness after the riots and it carried over."

In a local newspaper interview Chief Streicher said the police were experiencing a "tough time."

"They're just not feeling a lot of support," he said.

Mr. Fangman, the union chief, said that officers had "been afraid to take enforcement action in black neighborhoods," contending that they faced a "lynch-mob mentality" by local politicians and the news media.

"It's not a physical fear," Mr. Fangman said of the officers. "They are simply hesitant for fear of being labeled a racist, especially if it's a white officer." [Clines, 2001]

Of course, the consequences of this were also what could be expected:

During this period, there has been a six-fold increase in shooting incidents citywide, with all but one victim black, further polarizing the city since the three days of confrontations in April between black protesters and the police.

"We're seeing an epidemic rise in violent crime," said Keith A. Fangman, the president of the Fraternal Order of Police union.

Since the protests, there have been 59 shooting incidents in the city with 77 gunshot victims, compared with 9 shootings and 11 victims in the comparable three months last year.

"The aftermath of the riots has actually been more harmful to the city than the riots themselves," Mr. Fangman said. [ibid.]

Nor was this phenomenon limited to Cincinnati. Media reports from around that time located it in a number of other cities, includ-ing Los Angeles (Hale, 2001) Seattle (Tizon & Forgrave, 2001), and

London, as well as other areas in the UK (Bamber & Bisset, 2000; Johnston, 2001)

The case of Seattle was particularly noteworthy. There, after being vilified over the killing by a policeman of a black man who was dragging the officer's partner with a car, the police noticeably slackened their efforts. This is from the above-mentioned report in the *Seattle Times*:

> The cops on the street have different names for it: de-policing, selective disengagement, tactical detachment. They even joke about it, calling themselves "tourists in blue."
>
> Whatever the term, rank-and-file officers in the Seattle Police Department say it is a spreading phenomenon in the city's black neighborhoods, and a logical reaction to chronic charges of police racism.
>
> De-policing is passive law enforcement: Officers consciously stop trying to prevent low-level crime and simply react to 911 calls. Many officers, wary of being labeled racists or racial profilers, say they hold back or bypass opportunities to make traffic stops or arrests of black suspects.
>
> Black community leaders said yesterday they won't accept lax law enforcement; the police are paid to protect the public, even when it means taking heat.
>
> But several officers said caution on the streets is inevitable and will hurt black communities the most as crime increases in their neighborhoods.
>
> "It's real. It's happening," said Eric Michl, a Seattle patrol officer for 17 years. "Parking under a shady tree to work on a crossword puzzle is a great alternative to being labeled a racist and being dragged through an inquest, a review board, an FBI and U.S. Attorney's investigation and a lawsuit."

Not surprisingly, pursuit of the ego ideal having been denied to them, the motivation of police officers has shifted to minimizing the pursuit of promotion and recalculating the cost benefit ratio by seeking higher pay and minimizing their contributions, especially when those contributions are likely to get them into trouble. This was noted in an article in the *New York Times* (Butterfield, 2001):

Police departments in cities across the nation are facing what some call a personnel crisis, with the number of recruits at record lows, an increasing number of experienced officers turning down promotions to sergeant or lieutenant and many talented senior officers declining offers to become police chiefs, executive recruiters and police officials say.

Making the situation worse, in some cities a growing number of police officers are quitting for higher-paying jobs in suburban departments or private businesses.

These problems have come at a time when crime is at its lowest levels since the late 1960s and the police should be feeling good about themselves. But, the experts say, many officers from the lowest to the highest rank are questioning their occupation, tempted by higher pay in the private sector after a decade- long economic boom and discouraged by seemingly constant public and news media criticism about police brutality and racial profiling.

Of course, the level of crime was not likely to stay down, especially as experienced, highly qualified police officers cut down their motivational investment and decamped to areas where their cost–benefit ratio was likely to be better. In fact, everything else being equal, it could be confidently expected that the quality of police work would deteriorate, the charges of abuse would increase, and the situation would simply get worse.

For the purposes of this book, I checked the current situation in Cincinnati. This is from an article in *CityBeat*, which describes itself as "Cincinnati's News and Entertainment Weekly" (Osborne, 2006):

With homicides a near daily occurrence in Cincinnati and street shootings becoming bolder and more common, some city officials are beginning to question privately—and a few not so privately— whether more could be done to reduce violent crime.

Cincinnati has had 32 homicides so far this year as of May 8, putting the city on track to exceed last year's 79 homicides. 2005 was the city's deadliest year since 1971. . . .

Secret crime study

A tide of violence is sweeping the Queen City's streets, according to an independent study on police deployment issues. Several sources provided *CityBeat* data from the study, which has been completed but not publicly released.

The study shows that Cincinnati's homicide rate increased a staggering 190% between 2000 and 2004. In 2000, Cincinnati was listed as 111th among major urban areas in the USA for homicides per capita. That ranking jumped to twenty-third just four years later, the study says.

During the same period, the city's violent crime rate increased more than 31%. Cincinnati's rank skyrocketed from eighty-fifth among major urban areas in 2000 to thirty-sixth in 2004, statistics indicate . . .

Real-life experience of veteran police officers underscores some of the study's findings.

Police Lieutenant Colonel James Whalen has noticed a marked difference in the prevalence of guns since he began his career twenty-one years ago.

"At the time a Cincinnati police officer would catch somebody on the street with a gun on them four or five times a year," Whalen says. "Now it's four or five times a day. It's a massive change."

This increase in crime would be expected to have effects in a reluctance of its more affluent citizens to remain in the city, which would amplify the problem in various ways. For example, there would be a shrinkage of tax base and amenities, which would further exacerbate the problem That has certainly happened. Census figures in 2006 revealed that Cincinnati has been leading the nation's big cities in population loss, having shed 6.8% of its residents between 2000 and 2005. Fear of violent crime is widely cited as an important element in this decline (Klepal & Perry, 2006).

It would be absurd, of course, to suppose that all of this has been caused by the failure of politically correct city officials to support the police in 2001. None the less, if we can see that failure as emblematic of a generalized cultural breakdown along anti-Oedipal lines, the causality seems plausible enough.

The destruction of language

As its meaning shifts from Oedipal to anti-Oedipal, the idea of what the organization should be doing shifts further in the direction of taking its place, not within the framework of exchange, but within the political struggle against oppression. Organizations are increasingly likely to subordinate themselves to the mantras of their politics.

At the same time, they must appeal to the diminishing fraction who are still willing and able to do the organization's work, which means formulating their political principles in ways that will make sense in exchange terms. The result is likely to be an increasing incoherence in organizational discourse. In effect, organizational participants are being asked to believe two contradictory things. First, they must believe that the organization should be and is selectively enhancing the prospects of members of groups defined by their historical victimization. Second, they must believe that the organization is acting rationally within the framework of exchange, and, hence, that everyone is being evaluated on the basis of their contribution. Yet, there will be no possibility to clarify the meanings of this discourse, since to do so would reveal its incoherence, making it impossible for it to function, not to mention being politically incorrect in the sense of violating the principle of validating the sense of grievance.

I suggest that as the result of conundrums like this, language, within the anti-Oedipal organization, changes its nature. This destruction of language is perhaps the deepest form taken by organization self-destruction. The key to understanding this lies in an understanding of the nature of language. Language is perhaps the most fundamental element of the exchange process and is itself constituted out of exchange. Political correctness means the death of language in the sense that the exchange character of language is lost. It ceases to be a medium of communication and becomes instead a medium of concealment.

Consider a speech made by Hewlett-Packard CEO Carly Fiorina to a conference of high-tech executives. As reported in the San Jose *Mercury-News*, Fiorina said that Silicon Valley was falling short on diversity efforts because it was not a high enough priority.

> "The fact is that diversity is not a hiring practice or a hiring priority in many Silicon Valley companies," said Fiorina, speaking on a starstudded panel of high-tech executives who had been brought together at the San Jose Hyatt by the Rev. Jesse Jackson's Rainbow/ Push Coalition. "As a result, this industry has far too much conformity."

With a direct and stern demeanor on the podium, however, it was Fiorina who laid the responsibility for diversifying the workforce at the doorstep of her company.

Fiorina asked executives to look in the mirror and examine their companies' workforce. She scrutinized HP's faces and found it still falling short of ideals.

To stir HP's pot of innovation, she has made diversity the center-piece to her goal of reinventing the company.

"Diversity inspires creativity and inventiveness, and those are the core virtues of the New Economy," she said. [Kwan, 2000]

Fiorina's speech blends together three quite different meanings of the term "diversity". We may refer to them as *viewpoint diversity*, *ethnic diversity*, and *victim-group diversity*. With regard to the first meaning, diversity is taken to impart intellectual complexity at the level of the group. With this meaning of the term, Fiorina is on good grounds when she associates it with innovation and creativity. This is standard organization theory (e.g., Weick, 1969). But the idea that viewpoint diversity is something you can determine by "looking at" people holds only if you assume that it is closely correlated with ethnic diversity. Yet, even if we grant that questionable assumption, saying that the high-tech industry was not diverse was absurd. Silicon Valley was the very model of ethnic diversity. Silicon Valley start-ups at the time were headed by Asians, most notably Indians, in numbers far out of proportion to their representation in the population (Lewis, 2001).

But, of course, that was not what Fiorina had in mind. She was referring to the third sort of diversity, in which diversity is defined only with regard to membership in groups defined as having been oppressed. Victim group percentages are certainly lower in the high-tech industry than their share of the overall population. This is undoubtedly what she had in mind when "with a direct and stern demeanor" she "laid the responsibility for diversifying the work-force at the doorstep of her company".

If this was what she meant by diversity, though, it is difficult to tie it in with the sort of viewpoint diversity that she associated with innovation and creativity. For some of these groups the level of edu-cational attainment that would be necessary to participate in a rele-vant conversation is far below that of the rest of the population

(Thernstrom & Thernstrom, 1999). Yet, that is exactly what Fiorina did, even to the extent of saying that the high-tech industry, then the centre of the most creative outpouring of technological ideas in the history of the world, had "far too much conformity", a condition she was evidently going to deal with by making diversity "the centerpiece to her goal of reinventing the company".

Fiorina's speech is a hodge-podge of ideas that makes no sense, as anyone can see. It cannot be understood. But she has used this self-contradictory word-salad to define the way she is going to "reinvent the company", and she has made it clear that variation from these ideas, whatever they mean, will be taken as a sign of moral dereliction. So, what does one make of this, and especially what does one make of it if one is an employee of Hewlett-Packard?

That employee would understand from this that a certain form of speech has become obligatory, yet the ideas that the speech would be presumed to express are contradictory within themselves and cannot be thought. The words must be vocalized, and with enthusiasm, but it is the act of speech that has meaning, not the words themselves. The act is best understood as a form of concrete physical activity.

In his novel *1984*, George Orwell brings this forward in his discussion of "Newspeak". He says,

> The intention was to make speech, and especially speech on any subject not ideologically neutral, as nearly as possible independent of consciousness. For the purposes of everyday life it was no doubt necessary, or sometimes necessary, to reflect before speaking, but a Party member called upon to make a political or ethical judgment should be able to spray forth the correct opinions as automatically as a machine gun spraying forth bullets. . . . Ultimately it was hoped to make articulate speech issue from the larynx without involving the higher brain centres at all. [pp. 253–254]

Specifically, in a well-known passage, he refers to this as "duckspeak":

> As he watched the eyeless face with the jaw moving rapidly up and down, Winston had a curious feeling that this was not a real human being but some kind of dummy. It was not the man's brain that was speaking, it was his larynx. The stuff that was coming out of him

consisted of words, but it was not speech in the true sense: it was noise uttered in unconsciousness, like the quacking of a duck. [*ibid.*, p. 48]

What we see here is that public language has become a venue for ritualized displays. Words have become separated from meaning, which becomes private and increasingly inchoate (Kuran, 1995). The matter is worse than that, though. In political correctness, meanings become not only inchoate, but positively frightening, since they stand in opposition to what we are obliged to say, under threat of severe sanction. Introspection comes to be experienced as dangerous. This is a situation that begs to be resolved by projection, as when Fiorina addresses her audience "with a direct and stern demeanor".

In all this, the capacity language offers to compare and share our experience of reality becomes lost. It ceases to be an intersubjective structure, and becomes solipsistic. Political correctness needs no exchange, but requires the submission of one to the other. In the end, then, what appears to be language within political correctness is simply an invocation of the grandiose, primitive self of whoever has power, and does not recognize the existence of independent others. Language revolves around the desires of this "I". For the use of such "language", others are entirely dependent on the one who is saying "I", and this dependency must be the source of extreme slavishness and passivity, and the abandonment of moral and intellectual autonomy; one must give up one's own independent connection with reality. As a result, one has no choice but to idealize the powerful other and live in the hope that this other knows what he or she is doing and will take care of one.

From this comes the chorus of the sheep that Orwell invokes in *Animal Farm* (1945): "Two legs bad, four legs good". And notice that susceptibility to this degeneration is in no way diminished by intelligence, nor is it even necessarily mitigated by education, as we can clearly see. On the contrary, paraphrasing Alan Ginsburg, I can truly say that I have seen the best minds of my generation destroyed by political correctness.

At the same time, the language of the powerful other, who has been deprived of criticism and anything else that does not fit within his or her narcissism, also loses its intersubjective character and its capacity to mediate reality. The mind of this person must become an echo-chamber for his or her projections. As a result, the actions of this person must become increasingly unaccountable, arbitrary, and nonsensical.

This must have very serious consequences for the quality of organizational decisions anywhere that political correctness touches, which, as we can see in the case of Fiorina's redefinition of the company on the basis of "diversity", can become everywhere. Thought, which depends on language for its precision, becomes impossible. It becomes impossible, that is to say, to figure things out and it becomes impossible to refine one's thoughts by thinking about them.

An organization that operates this way would no longer be said to make conscious decisions at all, but only to move on the basis of unconscious forces. In truth, it could hardly be said to be an organization at all, any more than a mob is an organization. The process of organizational self-destruction would then be well on its way.

Conclusion

In concluding this chapter, we do well to recall that political correctness does not acknowledge limitation and does not lend itself to the reasonable resolution of the grievances that it champions. On the contrary, the very notion of reasonableness, and even that of reason, comes under its attack. The concept of victimization that it validates is not relative and defined with regard to a just order. It is absolute, and defined with regard to an unattainable ideal. Thus, it legitimates a war against everything that exists and even everything that could exist, all of which will always fall intolerably short and deserve to be destroyed. Ultimately, its spirit is nihilistic (Horowitz, 1998). This should give us cause to question the conviction of righteousness with which its aims are often pursued.

CHAPTER TWO

Organization and meaning: a multi-level psychoanalytic treatment of the Jayson Blair scandal at the *New York Times*

With Larry Hirschhorn

Understanding meaning

A common criticism of psychoanalytic theory is that it is reductionistic, that it seeks to explain phenomena at one level of analysis, for example, the social, by reference to concepts that are appropriate to another level, the individual. This critique is often legitimate, but it does not apply here.

The reason for this is that psychoanalytic theory, as used here, is a theory of symbolism. It is not so much about behaviour as about *the meaning of* behaviour, and the meaning of behaviour is essentially the same across levels of analysis. Take, for example, two responses to an event. A country is attacked. A young man responds by joining his country's armed forces; the country's government responds by beginning to convert its production facilities from consumer goods to war materiel. We have no problem seeing these two actions as having the same meaning, each appropriate to the level on which it is taken.

As this simple example illustrates, looking at levels of analysis in terms of meaning produces results that are quite different from more behaviourally orientated approaches. For psychoanalytic

theory, multi-level analysis is not a matter of finding causal relationships between different types of entities. Rather, it is a matter of
validating a general statement about the way a meaning is made by
finding that meaning at a number of levels. The point of multi-level
analysis, then, is not to provide a picture of the relations among
disparate phenomena, but to provide a richer understanding of one.
One may think of the result as polychromatic, each level of analysis presenting a picture of a single meaning through a lens of a
different colour.

One purpose of this chapter will be to validate this use of psychoanalytic theory by illustrating the way, as a theory of meaning,
it can contribute to the cross-level analysis of organizations. Larry
Hirschhorn and I will do so in a way that may seem paradoxical,
by showing a clash, a contestation about meaning. Two different
and competing ideas about the meaning of an organization, the
Oedipal and the anti-Oedipal, will help to give clarity to one
another, and the clash between these meanings will be used to
explain the behaviour at each level.

The organization we will analyse at these various levels is
the *New York Times*. We will look at the *Times* with a focus upon the
peculiar case of Jayson Blair, a reporter who was found to have
been plagiarizing and fabricating material, and the *Times'* treatment
of him.

The scope of Blair's fraud

On 6 June 2003, Howell Raines, the executive editor of the *New York
Times*, and his managing editor, Gerald Boyd, met with their staff to
announce their resignations. Over the preceding weeks, the *Times*
had itself revealed that one of its reporters, Jayson Blair, had fabricated sources and quotes as well as plagiarized other newspapers.
In a candid post mortem, the *Times* noted on 11 May 2003,

> Ten days ago, Jayson Blair resigned as a reporter for the *New York
> Times* after the discovery that he had plagiarized parts of an article
> on April 26 about the Texas family of a soldier missing in Iraq. An
> article on Page 1 today recounts a chain of falsifications and plagia-
> rism that unraveled when the *Times* began an inquiry into that

Texas article. At least 36 more articles written by Mr Blair since October reflected plagiarism, misstatements, misrepresentation of the reporter's whereabouts or a combination of those . . . Spot checks of the 600 articles he had written over the prior four years have found other apparent fabrications, and that inquiry continues. [*New York Times*, 2003]

Moreover, as the *Times* reporters indicated, people had been aware of Blair's extremely sloppy reporting and his disregard for accuracy for at least three years, but the paper had not dismissed him. Instead, he had been given many second chances and at one point was transferred to the sports department for training in accuracy. Alex S. Jones, a former *Times* reporter and the co-author of *The Trust: The Private and Powerful Family Behind the New York Times* (Tifft & Jones, 1999), commented,

To the best of my knowledge, there has never been anything like this at the *New York Times* . . . There has never been a systematic effort to lie and cheat as a reporter at the *New York Times* comparable to what Jayson Blair seems to have done. [Barry, Barstow, Glater, Liptak, & Steinberg, 2003]

People wondered, reasonably, if Blair's identity as an African-American male, combined with the *Times'* and Raines' commitment to diversity, explained Blair's seeming immunity. They wondered whether political correctness prevented criticism of Blair, and made it impossible for the organization to exert the usual control over him. (e.g., Boehlert, 2003).

We believe that those who asked these questions were correct, but that giving a positive answer here is only the beginning of the story. It sees the story as taking place only at the level of organizational process. For a more complete understanding of this occurrence, it is necessary to examine the workings of political correctness at all levels.

As we have seen, political correctness is a manifestation of anti-Oedipal psychology; it creates an attack on the idea of objective reality, and, hence, of objective truth. If white heterosexual patriarchy is suspect, its claim to represent the truths of our lives is suspect. Instead, every culture is seen as having its own truth. The very idea of an objective truth is a way in which the dominant group represses the cultures whose truth is different from theirs. One may easily imagine that this will have a considerable impact on an organization like the *New York Times*, whose business has always been defined by taking the paternal role within the Oedipal function, and reporting the objective truth. It would be replaced by a maternal orientation, nurturing the oppressed group and defending its own truth, which would be defined by its feeling of being oppressed by the ideas of the dominant group.

We will look at the institutional, individual, group, intrapsychic, and organizational levels, and at the level of the organization's relationship to its environment. The working of political correctness in this case is augmented by understanding the way the tension between Oedipal and anti-Oedipal meanings played out at each of these levels.

A multilevel analysis of a clash of meanings

The institutional level

As the "paper of record", the *New York Times* has had a unique and important place in the structure of meaning in American society. It is relied upon to offer objective accounts of the important facts of the time, and, indeed, is even relied upon to offer an objective appraisal of what facts are important. An institution whose words can be relied upon to present an objective picture of what is real makes it possible for people to plan their lives with confidence, to understand what their obligations are and to accept them, and to act in a way that makes it possible for their behaviour to be understood and co-ordinated with the behaviour of others. Now, the paternal function stands for the objective world in which truths, however uncomfortable, have standing. This suggests that the *New York Times* is a singular component, a bulwark, of the paternal function. It is the father of fathers.

Of course, the *Times* has never been perfect. The best of human institutions are still human and humans make mistakes. But, within the context of its responsibility, this fact has translated into a demand, which the paper has made upon itself, to be obsessive in its drive for accuracy, ruthless in its error correction, and to make sure that everyone in its employ makes these demands upon them-selves. (For our present purpose, the case of Walter Duranty, a Pulitzer Prize winning *Times* reporter who covered the Soviet Union during Stalin's time and presented a picture far more sympa-thetic than the facts warranted, will be considered an aberration. Within this perspective, the *Times'* credulity is understandable, first on the basis of ignorance—he was, after all, the person who had the job of informing them—and then by a nostalgic attachment to its own past. Of course, there was also, undoubtedly, a romantic attachment to the idea of "revolution" abroad in American society at the time. From our perspective, this is simply an indication that the appeal of a fusion that can be attained through the destruction of the father has deep roots. On the other hand, there can be no doubt that Stalin, representing the "dictatorship of the proletariat", was also taking the role of a father. What is unique about our own time is the dominance of the belief that society can do without what the father represents.)

This, of course, is what makes the Blair case so interesting. The intellectual issue is not built around the fact that Blair committed journalistic sins. In truth, there has been an epidemic of that in recent times. The interesting question is how the *Times* could have let him keep his position in the face of clear evidence that he had been making mistakes, fabricating events, and even plagiarizing. Our answer will be that the demands imposed by the *Times* only make sense within Oedipal psychology. In anti-Oedipal psychol-ogy, they are redefined as impositions and agencies of oppression. Blair, as the member of a group that has been deprived of love in the past, is entitled to be compensated with love for being subjected to this oppression.

The drama of Blair, therefore, is a clash between systems of meaning. It took place at many levels. All reflected the widest possi-ble struggle between Oedipal and anti-Oedipal impulses in the culture.

The individual level

To study organizations at the level of the individual, one does best to look at the leaders, and the way they define their organizational roles. In the case of the *Times*, we are fortunate to have a way of studying the transformation in the orientation towards the father because we can see differences in the way that the father and son defined the central role of publisher.

The *New York Times* is an operation of the Ochs-Sulzberger family and has been since its inception. The role of publisher has passed from a member of one generation to another. Most recently, it passed from Arthur Hayes Sulzberger, Jr, known as Punch, to Arthur Ochs Sulzberger Jr, known, not without condescension, as Pinch. In the traditional Oedipal process, the son subordinates himself to the father, while in the anti-Oedipal configuration, the son gains meaning by refusing this subordination. This difference is very much on display in the Sulzberger succession at the *Times*.

Subordination to the father means internalizing the meanings and values he represents. In the case of an organizational succession, it would mean commitment to the meanings and values of the organization. Given the position of the *Times* in our society, it is easy to see that this subordination would be seen as a sacred trust. One reason that the *Times* has been such a stellar newspaper is that past and present family members who have owned it subordinated their personal interests to the *Times'* excellence as an institution. They have reinvested much of their earnings in the paper rather than distribute them as profits. In their study of the family, Tifft and Jones (1999, p. 585) note that in 1986, the four Sulzberger children (one son and three daughters of Arthur Sr and Iphigene Sulzberger) and their thirteen children

> pledged never to sell the critical voting class B shares of the company stock outside the family. Any family member who wanted to redeem his or her class B stock for cash had to offer it to the family or to the *New York Times* Company first. Before the stock could be sold to any outsider it had to be converted into ordinary Class A stock. The covenant bound them to these terms until twenty-one years after the death of the longest lived descendant of Iphigene who was alive at the time the agreement was executed.

They go on to note that, by signing the document and executing the agreement, the Sulzbergers gave up their chance to earn the fortune that would have come to them through the sale of class B stock, which provides control over the company.

A lawyer who drew up the documents told the children that "the hypothetical windfall from selling the Class B stock could be a billion dollars or more." Yet, they weren't the least bit tempted to preserve their option to do so. [*ibid.*, p. 623]

Family members also subordinated themselves psychologically to the *Times* as an institution.

The Sulzbergers had been taught from birth never to think of themselves as rich or powerful. At the funeral of Iphigene Sulzberger, Susan Dryfoos, a granddaughter eulogized her by calling the newspaper a "trust" and "a tradition that is far greater than any single individual." Publicly, Susan pledged her generation to "carry on" and to "be humble." "No swelled heads," she promised her grandmother. "Our memory of you will keep us straight." [*ibid.*, pp. 628–629]

Subordination also characterized the way in which "Punch" Sulzberger, the son of Arthur, Sr and the father of "Pinch", took up his role as publisher. He held his character as a person in reserve. Not unlike royalty, he underlined the distinction between the office and the person. He took his role as given by its place in the objective order and directed his behaviour in accordance with what he believed were the interests of the organization. On the one side, this could lead people to experience him as detached, but on the other, it gave people the confidence that he was acting on behalf of the institution rather than in response to the pressure of personal needs. As one family member noted,

He was smart enough at some point in his life to realize that people foam around the publisher of the *New York Times*, and if you're not careful they're all biting at you or sucking at you, licking at you. It suited Punch's character and personality to remain this rigid person unto himself and never let very much of himself out to anybody. [*ibid.*, p. 596]

As a result,

He never involved himself directly in stories and only rarely in editorials. When he read a news article that displeased him he complained to the top editor and to him alone, never to the individual reporter, It was his way of keeping the publisher's authority in reserve, like a vast untapped store of gold bullion. [*ibid.*, p. 597]

As one company executive noted, "When you're before him you know you're before the institution" (*ibid.*, p. 597).

But if the older Sulzberger defined his role by subordination, the younger did just the opposite.

Arthur Ochs Sulzberger Jr, born in 1951, was a baby-boomer and a child of the 1960s. Raised by his mother, he had been very influenced by his experiences in "Outward Bound", an organization that enables people to test their limits, their courage, and their interpersonal skills in rugged outdoor activities. Evidently, through this experience, he learned to trust his own spontaneity. Like many of his generation, he was committed to bringing more of that spontaneity to his role.

> Arthur Jr.'s office on the eleventh floor of the *Times* Building was similarly a stylistic counterpoint to his father's. Punch's complex of rooms communicated unostentatious tradition and a comfortable dowdiness; Arthur Jr.'s office conveyed modernity and informality. His desk, reaching across an expanse of blue wall-to-wall carpeting, was sleek and modular, at one end stood his computer, the only terminal at the paper able to access both the news and the business operations—with an eye popping Star Trek screen saver. . . . On a side table sat an orange model motorcycle with a helmeted rider and sidecar, a reminder of the sidecar Arthur Jr. had once owned in London. Across the room, above the dark stained wooden reading easel was a large movie poster advertising John Wayne in "The Sands of Iwo Jima"—an odd choice for a person who so consciously disdained the traditional macho stereotype. Visitors were startled to see the publisher of the *New York Times* don a headset and answer his incoming calls with a curt "Sulzberger" or fling his leg over the arm of his chair as though he were watching television. Except for photos of past publishers and immediate family members, the only touch of tradition was a loudly ticking ship's clock by Seth Thomas. [*ibid.*, p. 654]

This informal style of taking up a role is by now a familiar one. It reflects the heritage of the generation that matured in the 1960s. Its members are now in leadership roles throughout the economy and society. Considered by itself, it has real strengths. It can support more direct and truthful talk, it acknowledges and draws on people's individual passions, and it reduces some of the psychological injuries associated with status and class difference. On the other hand, it can become dangerous when spontaneous desire is meant as a protest against social control. Organizations succeed by allocating scarce resources to selected ends. Desire can animate work, but must be subordinated to organizational choice. In the context of organizations, this means that an insistence on spontaneity can become an attack against hierarchy and the authority it represents. Under these conditions, it takes on an anti-Oedipal meaning. Then, in accordance with the meanings assigned by political correctness, the attack against hierarchy and authority becomes redefined as part of the struggle of the oppressed against the oppressors.

Arthur's suspicion of hierarchy was clear. It also appears that it is categorical, and does not make the necessary distinction between hierarchy that expresses rational authority and hierarchy that does not. For example, in 1992, he told a journalist,

> Some argue that fear is an inherent by-product of any structure based in hierarchy. I can't swear that's true, but I suspect it is. And if it is true our course is clear. For the *New York Times* to become all it can be and for it to flourish in the years ahead, we must reduce our dependency on hierarchy in decision making of every sort. [Auletta, 1993, p. 56]

One would expect this stance to undermine Arthur's ability to exercise legitimate authority, and, hence, the objective role of publisher, where it was most needed. This appears to have been the case.

For example, it is a commonplace of the newspaper business that there is tension between the editors and the business executives, with editors asking for more resources to improve the paper's quality and business executives, focused on profits, asking the editors to do with less. The publisher, at the top of hierarchy, typically acts as the court of last resort as he or she works to integrate the twin goals of quality and profit. This role, which we may understand as being an expression of the paternal function, is important because when the publisher does the work of integration, each side is free to pursue its particular objective with passion and focus. The publisher, by contrast, is required to take the objective stance and is precluded from the whole-hearted commitment his subordinates are entitled to, which, in fact, allows them a certain organizational "innocence". Instead, the publisher has to integrate conflicting objectives alone. This is also why we characterize the chief executive as "lonely at the top". This was the premise under which Punch took up his role. But, for his son, with his antagonism toward hierarchy and authority, the exercise of this integrative function became extremely problematic.

> He had watched his father play the role of court of last resort at the paper. He didn't want to spend the next twenty years of his life refereeing every conflict that came along between the newsroom and the business departments. [Tifft & Jones, 1999, p. 647]

For a final point of contrast, consider a commencement speech given by the younger Sulzberger (2006) to the 2006 graduating class of the State University of New York at New Paltz, which is available at their website. He said, in part,

> I'll start with an apology.
>
> When I graduated from college in 1974, my fellow students and I had just ended the war in Vietnam and ousted President Nixon. Okay, that's not quite true. Yes, the war did end and yes, Nixon did resign in disgrace—but maybe there were larger forces at play.
>
> Either way, we entered the real world committed to making it a better, safer, cleaner, more equal place. We were determined not to repeat the mistakes of our predecessors. We had seen the horrors and futility of war and smelled the stench of corruption in government.
>
> Our children, we vowed, would never know that.
>
> So, well, sorry. It wasn't supposed to be this way.
>
> You weren't supposed to be graduating into an America fighting a misbegotten war in a foreign land.
>
> You weren't supposed to be graduating into a world where we are still fighting for fundamental human rights, be it the rights of immigrants to start a new life; the rights of gays to marry; or the rights of women to choose.

You weren't supposed to be graduating into a world where oil still drives policy and environmentalists have to relentlessly fight for every gain.

You weren't. But you are. And for that I'm sorry.

Obviously, in this speech, Sulzberger was expressing an identification with his cohort and his commitment to the politically correct, anti-Oedipal political position often identified with it. By itself, the fact that he held a certain political position need not have directly affected the operations of the *Times*, even if he took personal responsibility, as he did, for the attainment of certain political outcomes. But even if that were so, he was making the speech as the publisher of the *Times* and a person might easily have come away with the idea that his political view might carry some weight at the *Times* and be reflected in its coverage. That would call the objectivity of the *Times* into question and undermine its institutional significance. It is impossible to imagine that the older Sulzberger would have made that speech.

We now turn to the way the conflict between Oedipal and anti-Oedipal played out at the group level.

The group level

Consider a series of failed executive retreats that Sulzberger Jr sponsored from October of 1992 through January of 1993. He hoped that, through the work of the retreats, the two sides of the company would agree on a statement of values and mission so that he would no longer have to act as the court of last resort. One can see anti-Oedipal meaning operating here. The statement would represent the dissolution of differences and boundaries between the functions; hence, there would be no conflicts between them. The newspaper, like the idealized family, would be harmonious, governed by the maternal function.

But this fantasy is precisely why the retreats he sponsored failed. The laborious work of producing mission and value statements did not dissolve differences; indeed, it could not, because the differences and boundaries between the functions were objectively necessary and real. Instead, the retreats gave voice to the hostility of both sides as well as anger at Arthur. After one difficult session, participants asked him, "why did you drag us here?" (Auletta, 1993, p. 64)

Consider an episode during one of the retreats. It reveals in microcosm the links between authority, hierarchy, work, and passion. Sulzberger hired a facilitator to help the editorial leadership and the business executives create a shared mission statement for the company. The retreat's facilitator is at the centre of this reported episode but, by examining his actions, we can also see again how Sulzberger was taking up his leadership role. Indeed, Sulzberger himself pointed out that when the retreat participants attacked the facilitator, they were, in fact, attacking him (*ibid.*).

On the morning of the second day of the retreat, the facilitator began by asking participants to discuss their statement of values but "then jarred everyone by changing the subject and encouraging people to speak candidly about their frustrations in the newsroom, about the fear, about the authoritarianism". The journalist goes on to note,

> When they resisted, Sulzberger himself weighed in, describing his own unhappiness with communications at the paper. He challenged [executive editor] Max Frankel and his staff to practice bottom up rather than top down management, to open themselves to change, to be well,—*nicer.* [*ibid.*, p. 62]

They should, in our terms, become maternal.

When participants still hesitated to talk about their fear and frustration, the facilitator suggested that they describe the "rules of the road" that defined the culture of the newsroom

> "When in doubt, dissemble," was a rule that one editor cited. "Paradox: the best newspaper in the world can't keep its bathrooms clean," was another editor's contribution. Each remark was written on the board for a total of thirty items. Frankel exploded "let's not play stupid games. This is intellectually dishonest. This doesn't represent what we think of ourselves." [*ibid.*, p. 64]

When the facilitator suggested that they break up into small groups, "Frankel, cried out, 'Stop all this mindless clamor for change, change, change! Let's get specific. Let's put the problems on the table and work to solve them'" (*ibid.*). The result was that Frankel felt attacked and his subordinates embarrassed.

The reader familiar with group process can recognize what the facilitator was doing. When asked to discuss their values, executives are frequently at a loss, because the discourse feels abstract, at one remove from the business issues and problems of work that motivate them daily. Facing then what was probably a passive, if not wary, group, the facilitator sought to create fireworks by exposing the paternal authority figure, in this case Frankel, to attack. This was the meaning of his question about the "rules of the road". People in groups always feel ambivalent about the authority figure, even a "good" one. Their passion is for their work, so their appreciation for his leadership is always tinged with anger because of the resources they have been denied. It is these passions that establish the only sure foundation for intensity and heat. But, of course, these passions, when first expressed, will initially increase the level of conflict between the two sides. As a result the facilitator is called upon to work at his "personal best".

However, facilitators sometimes rely on this ambivalence, rarely with much awareness, to take an anti-Oedipal route. They mobilize an attack on the authority figure, the father, as if getting him out of the way were all that would be necessary for people to be able to do exactly what they desire. In so doing, they shortcut the more difficult task of helping people engage their passions for the work itself, within its real and necessary organizational limitations. This is why Frankel exploded in frustration. Using the short cut described here, the facilitator thus avoids his own work. Ironically, when the group attacks the authority figure they feel regret and shame, and then turn on the facilitator for exposing them to a regressed group process. Indeed, after the retreat, group members felt angry with both the facilitator and Arthur, who, after all, had hired him, and with whom he was evidently identified.

This incident enacts in microcosm the important links between authority, work, and passion. The facilitator distances himself from the passions associated with the work itself. As a result, he withdraws from his own work of facilitating inter-group conflict. Lacking a harness for work, neither the facilitator nor the participants are engaged, so the facilitator attacks authority, leading first to heat, but later to feelings of shame.

These connections suggest that Sulzberger, with whom the facilitator was identified, in so far as he also attacked the principle of authority, was himself wary of engaging his subordinates around the passions associated with their work. In other words, he was not ready to take on the paternal function. This, again, is why he shied away from being the "court of last resort". It represents the clash between the anti-Oedipal and the Oedipal dynamic. The movement against authority within the group has no apparent meaning beyond itself. It is an attack upon authority for the sake of an attack upon authority. And, again, those who were invested in authority through the Oedipal dynamic felt attacked by it and hated it. Recall again what Frankel said: "let's not play stupid games. This is intellectually dishonest. This doesn't represent what we think of ourselves".

Now, an argument of this sort may carry conviction to the psychoanalytic student of group process, but it may be less convincing to someone else, who may well say that a retreat is an artificial setting, and that what happens there may have nothing to do with what is going on in the organization as such. In this case, though, we are fortunate in being able to see these same dynamics play out in a group setting that was very much a part of the organization as such.

Howell Raines, the executive editor of the newspaper at that time, held a town-hall meeting to discuss his handling of Jayson Blair. The meeting ended badly, with the staff attacking Raines. But Sulzberger enacted the same role at this meeting—attacking the leader—that he supported at the retreat. After the meeting, participants complained that he did not convene the meeting with dignity. They described in harsh terms how Arthur conducted himself. As one participant asked,

> Why hold a meeting where it was certain to become a spectacle. Or say, when asked his opinion of the situation, something as coarse and inarticulate as "it sucks?" Or not put on a necktie? Or worst of all, reach into a paper bag and take out a stuffed toy moose—apparently a tool out of some management manual, symbolizing the "moose in the room," that nobody wants to talk about, used to loosen things up—and hand it to a perplexed Raines? [Margolick, 2003, p. 143]

This person is suggesting that Arthur behaved disrespectfully, in a manner not befitting his "office". It makes sense to suggest that, by behaving this way, Sulzberger encouraged the others to behave disrespectfully to Raines. Handing the moose to a perplexed Raines certainly suggests that Raines was the fact that nobody wanted to talk about. He was identifying Raines as the father and authorizing an attack against him. This may be why the participants' fury was uninhibited and what gave reporters licence to attack the *Times* and Raines on unrelated websites—an assault that the family, as protector of the newspaper's reputation, could hardly tolerate. This would also explain why Maureen Dowd, a columnist for the *Times*, said that the attack on Raines reminded her of the novel, *Lord of the Flies*, in which young boys, in the absence of adults, formed groups that engaged in primitive and destructive behaviour (*ibid.*). This, in turn, suggests that the staff was trying to express regret for their destructive, patricidal behaviour when Raines, at a subsequent meeting, announced his resignation.

The intrapsychic level

Whatever it is as a social psychology, psychoanalytic theory is certainly a theory about what is going on in the individual psyche. So, we may look to find the same tensions within the minds of the individual members of the organization. We may think of this as the intrapsychic level of organizational analysis. Of most interest here is the mind of Jayson Blair.

In the course of the scandal, much attention was paid to Blair's position as an affirmative action hire, who was kept in place in the pursuit of diversity goals, and whose shortcomings could not be mentioned because of political correctness. These are correct, and we will discuss this below. But leaving the matter there would miss out on another important dimension, and perhaps the most interesting. That was the significance of the experience in the mind of Jayson Blair.

There, to begin with, the anti-Oedipal dynamic is clearly evident. For example, he titles his memoir of the incident *Burning Down my Masters' House* (Blair, 2004), and he said in an interview shortly after his discovery, "So Jayson Blair the human being could live," . . . "Jayson Blair the journalist had to die" (Pappu, 2003).

It would be easy to think of this statement as having a political meaning; that he was asserting his black self against the inherent racism of the *Times*. But the statement he made immediately before this suggests that this political meaning is only part of it, and arguably the least interesting:

> "I was young at the *New York Times*," said Mr. Blair. "I [*sic*] under a lot of pressure. I was black at the *New York Times*, which is something that hurts you as much as it helps you. I certainly have health problems, which probably led to me having to kill Jayson Blair, the journalist. I was either going to kill myself or I was going to kill the journalist persona." [*ibid.*]

But, as his memoir makes plain, the health problems he was referring to were problems of self-esteem, which, he believed, derived from the pressure he was facing and which, in turn, he felt, led to his alcoholism and drug addiction. But the pressure he was under came from the demands made on him by the *Times*. They arose from its paternal function.

It is clear from Blair's memoir that these demands and pressures were not seen as part of its institutional nature. In Blair's mind, the institutional position of the *New York Times* had no place. It was a sham and a charade. His primary experience of the *Times* seems to have been as an assault against his self-esteem. Blair saw the *Times* as the father, but this was a father defined within anti-Oedipal psychology, not Oedipal. This would be an illegitimate father, a father without the paternal function. The route to the ego ideal would not involve becoming like father, in the sense of working for the *Times*; rather, the *Times* was felt to be depriving him of the ego ideal. Others who worked for the *Times* were not models for emulation, but were the objects of his envy and resentment.

Consider his thoughts during the period when he was first being introduced to people as a regular employee, after having been at the *Times* as an intern:

> "Good luck," she added, beginning to turn away. "One more thing, Jayson. Congratulations on getting the chance to write for the *Times*."

> That pride, in some employees, emerged as snobbery and arrogance. The *Times* newsroom was a place where you could close your eyes, and in the words of one reporter, throw a ball and have a good chance of hitting an Ivy Leaguer who'd pretend not to know

your name. This was much more apparent upon my re-entry, and even many of the people who were kind to me seemed infused with the notion the *Times* was made up of the smartest journalists working on the planet. [Blair, 2004, p. 96]

Blair is, no doubt, correct that *Times* journalists consider themselves the best journalists on the planet, and that this is a source of great pride. This would come out of their participation in the shared belief in the singular institutional significance of the *Times*, and the belief that they were living up to it. But living up to it would mean living up to its demands. If those demands were not granted legitimacy and internalized, they would be seen as impositions. One would feel no pride in living up to them. Pride on the part of others would appear anomalous and would not be seen to have a legitimate basis. For that reason, the *Times* journalists' pride could only be seen as arrogance and personal affront. Here it is again:

My actions had tarnished the one thing that mattered to so many of them: the pride and respect they got for having their name on a *Times* business card and being able to mention at parties that they worked at the glorious *New York Times*. [*ibid.*, p. 56]

In the absence of a perceived paternal function, the only legitimate function of the paper would be maternal: to love and take care of him, defending him against the oppressive father. Failure to do that, as by making demands, would be seen as an act of badness on the organization's part. Blair makes little allowance for the objective situation the *Times* faced in the disaster he caused. Consider this exchange, which took place after he had checked into a mental hospital as the scandal of his plagiarism was getting its first exposure:

A friend at the *Times* had tried to convince me to stay in the hospital at least until the May 11 story was published. The friend had also asked me . . . whether I had considered helping the team of *Times* reporters on the story sort out some of the more murky details.

"I think you should consider it, Jayson. I mean, otherwise, the ramp-up from you being a troubled guy who made some mistakes to Journalistic Antichrist is about to jump from zero to fifty come Sunday."

"Do you think they would be willing to wait for me to get out of the hospital?" I asked. "I really have to put my health first, and they are not ready to release me."

"I totally understand that, but as a gesture of professional courtesy to your colleagues who have been asked to dig into the life of someone they sat by for several years, you might want to consider helping them. At least make sure they have covered all the problem stories," he said.

"I don't know, I have not even thought about it yet," I replied. "I have sort of blocked out the details of everything apart from the Texas story. I am just trying to stabilize. Do you think that they would be willing to wait until I get out of the hospital? . . . I know I shouldn't say this, but I have spent the last four years doing things on the *Times's* schedule . . ."

"Look, man, they shouldn't let you dictate the timing of the story . . ."

"My health has to come first," I interrupted . . .

I was exasperated.

"I am leaving whenever the doctors tell me to." [*ibid.*, p. 52, reprinted with the permission of Phoenix Books, Inc.]

Blair evidently does not believe that the *Times'* necessities, which grow out of its paternal function, create legitimate demands. Instead, he seems to feel abused by them. The *Times* should act as his mother, taking care of and nursing him in his pain.

According to our theory, the rejection of the father is, at the same time, the substantiation of the primitive fantasy of the return to primary narcissism. This is very much on view here. Blair is remarkably free in his expression of his fantasies.

For instance, in relation to his girlfriend, Zuza:

I would call Zuza on her cell phone, and . . . she would secretly arrange for me to be picked up and taken somewhere no one would find me. She would visit me there, and hold me, comforting me as she had done over the past few days in a way I felt no hospital or medications could.

We would live happily ever after, traveling to places like Africa and Southeast Asia, writing, painting and doing volunteer work. Then we would have two children together—one a boy and one a girl—

and we would give them exotic names, and raise them using the best of the parenting tools from both of our families—my mom and dad's love and tenderness combined with the independence and intellectual strength she gained from her parents. We would grow old together, having accomplished many important things that would change the world, and we would have done it in the most exciting of ways; our actions and our partnership being an inspiration to millions. [*ibid.*, p. 35, reprinted with the permission of Phoenix Books, Inc.]

This is a straightforward expression of the ego ideal: a fantasy of being with the perfect mother, a protector, a lover, someone who represents a world that revolves around Jayson with love, and in which Jayson will only have to do what he wants and he will be loved for it.

Now, of course, the ego ideal is critical in giving meaning to our lives, and whatever has meaning for us is associated with the ego ideal. What is interesting about Blair is not that he has an ego ideal, but that the ego ideal is tied to the escape from work. Work is not the pursuit of the ego ideal, but a barrier to its attainment. Evidently, Blair held the *Times* responsible for depriving him of the ego ideal, in just the same way that the infant saw the father as depriving it of its intimate connection with mother.

This leads to the view that Blair saw his plagiarism as a kind of retaliation. This is suggested by his lack of remorse, and by an apparent joy and pride as the scandal started to unfold. This is best seen in the interview he gave to the *New York Observer*:

"That was my favorite," Jayson Blair said. It was the morning of Monday, May 19, and the disgraced former NYT reporter was curled in a butterfly chair in his sparsely furnished Brooklyn apartment. He was eating a bagel and talking about one of his many fabricated stories—his March 27 account, datelined Palestine, W.Va., of Pvt. Jessica Lynch's family's reaction to their daughter's liberation in Iraq.

Mr. Blair hadn't gone to Palestine, W.Va. He'd filed from Brooklyn, N.Y. As he'd done before, he cobbled facts and details from other places and made some parts up. He wrote how Private Lynch's father had "choked up as he stood on the porch here overlooking the tobacco fields and cattle pastures."

That was a lie. In the *Times'* lengthy May 11 account of Mr. Blair's long trail of deception, it reported that "the porch overlooks no such thing."

Mr. Blair found this funny.

"The description was just so far off from reality," he said. "The way they described it in the *Times* story—someone read a portion of it for me. I just couldn't stop laughing."

And:

Through his rise, he made mistakes—a lot of them. Most, he said, were the result of the usual forces: bad information from the police, deadline pressure. And yet Mr. Blair felt that he deserved to keep on climbing. He grew frustrated with the metro grind, and admitted he became a problem in the newsroom. He claimed he was assigned to "idiot" editors and, as a result, "began to act out." He started being frequently absent and unavailable, he said, in a "misguided attempt to punish them." [*ibid.*]

The interpersonal level

We will turn in a moment to the institutional level of analysis, but, before doing so, there is a matter on the interpersonal level that comes up in connection with Blair's belief that the *Times* should mother him, which was that it was evidently shared by others.

The conversation Blair held from the hospital continued with this: "We ended the conversation with the atypical 'I love yous' [*sic*] that men do not normally share among themselves, and agreed to disagree" (Blair, 2004, p. 52, reprinted with the permission of Phoenix Books, Inc.).

What is fascinating here are the "I love yous". They suggest that Blair's colleague emotionally backed him, even while expressing the *Times'* position. If Blair is to be believed on this, it was characteristic of the employee response. That this would be true of his friends may not be surprising, although their closeness could easily have led to feelings of betrayal. But it seems to have been true even of those without a close personal relationship with him. For example, this is from Blair's report of a phone call from Zuza, after Blair had resigned in the face of mounting evidence of his transgressions:

"The strangest thing just happened. Gerald Boyd [then the *Times* managing editor] called me and told me to leave work."

"What?" I asked.

"He told me to leave work and go find you, to be with you, that you would need me. And then he came up to my desk and asked me to go find you." [ibid., p. 27, reprinted with the permission of Phoenix Books, Inc.]

Thus, Blair thought of himself as having been wounded by the demands of the *Times* and his colleagues, and even superiors, at the *Times* responded to him on that basis. Their response was maternal. They wanted to take care of him.

It is striking that Blair's colleagues at the *Times* would back him emotionally. The premise of our multi-level analysis suggests that we may find the same form of meaning at the level of the organization, to which we now turn.

The organizational level

The most striking feature of the Blair story is the extraordinary leniency shown Blair throughout his tenure at the *Times*. In November of 1999, shortly after his hire, he was assigned to police work but told his reporting was sloppy. In the fall of 2000, as the *Times* own investigation of the Blair incident noted, "Many newsroom colleagues say he also did brazen things, including delighting in showing around copies of confidential *Times* documents". In January of 2001, the metropolitan editor, Mr Landman, opposed Blair's promotion to full-time reporter, but he did not protest the move because, as he said later, "The publisher and the executive editor . . . had made clear the company's commitment to diversity—'and properly so'". In September of 2001, he wrote an article sufficiently laden with errors that it "required a correction so extensive that it attracted the attention of the new executive editor, Howell Raines". In January 2002, the metropolitan editor sent Mr. Blair "a sharply worded evaluation, noting that his correction rate was 'extraordinarily high by the standards of the paper'. He forwarded copies of that evaluation to two senior editors along with a note that read, 'There's big trouble I want you both to be aware of'". In April 2002, the same metropolitan editor sent off "a two-sentence e-mail message to newsroom administrators that read: 'we have to stop Jayson from writing for the *Times*. Right now.'" And the next day "[Blair] received a letter of reprimand and took a brief leave." Later that month, after agitating to get away from the metropolitan desk, the metropolitan editor "reluctantly signed off on a plan to send Mr. Blair to the sports department, although he recalled warning the sports editor: 'If you take Jayson, be careful'" (Barry, Barstow, Glater, Liptak, & Steinberg, 2003).

These events set the stage for his promotion! He was moved to the national desk and asked to help cover the sniper case in Washington, DC. His work there came under heavy fire for inaccuracy, but this did not prevent executive editor Howell Raines from congratulating him on his "gum shoe" reporting. He was subsequently assigned to cover the stories about Iraq that led to his exposure.

This extraordinary flow of events begs for explanation. We know how deeply ingrained the concept of the "newspaper of record" is for reporters at the *New York Times*. What powerful counter-idea could possibly lead them to betray the institution they so valued? We offer an explanation from the standpoint of anti-Oedipal psychology.

We can examine anti-Oedipal psychology at the organizational level by looking at the dynamic of "political correctness". As we have argued, political correctness (PC) is built around the image of maternal omnipotence and perfect benevolence, and around the rejection of the father, who is seen as having stolen the mother's love. The rules of PC, then, are that the father, identified as the white, heterosexual male, is to be hated, vilified, and denigrated. Those who are members of defined victim groups are entitled to be loved as compensation for the love he has stolen. The benevolence of the mother, and the contrasting malevolence of the father, give these dynamics the aspect of a moral struggle between the forces of goodness and those of badness.

What we can see from this is that the organization's function is redefined. On the one hand, in manifesting the attack upon the father, the organization turns against itself: against its hierarchy, as we have seen, and against the meaning of its work and its place within the paternal function. On the other hand, in its capacity as benevolent and loving mother, offering her love as compensation for that of which victims have been deprived, it takes on the role of a nurturer of victims: those outside and those within.

In the Oedipal dynamic, Blair's plagiarism and fabrication were real sins, in that they undermined the *Times'* responsibilities within the paternal function, which defined the meaning of the *Times*. In the anti-Oedipal dynamic, however, Blair's sins were reduced to minor transgressions, explainable as responses to the *Times* oppressive, unreasonable demands. Another meaning of the *Times* had emerged. In this new meaning, its role was to love Blair for the suffering he was subjected to by—the *New York Times*.

But notice that, redefined in this way, the meaning of work has nothing to do with the necessities of maintaining the organization. The focus of people's attention becomes the moral features of the organization itself, without regard to the work it has been established to do, and the value it provides to customers and clients.

For example, when he first took the publisher role, Sulzberger told a journalist "that his greatest challenge will be to bring more racial diversity and sexual equality to the paper" (Auletta, 1993, p. 60). What is striking about this statement is that Sulzberger did *not* say that his most serious challenge was to sustain the quality and excellence of the *Times' product*, while maintaining its economic viability. Yet, if he failed in these goals, the *Times* would ultimately go out of business and the goal of seeking diversity would be immaterial.

Similarly, in 2001 at the convention of the National Association of Black Journalists, Raines mentioned Blair in reference to the *Times'* effort to "spot and hire the best and brightest reporters on the way up", saying, "This campaign has made our staff better and, more importantly, more diverse" (Raines, 2003). Again, this statement reflects the redefinition: a diverse staff has become more important than a better staff.

We suggest that this transformation of meaning created the conditions for Jayson Blair's fraudulent activities. We can look at this in the context of a shift from "affirmative action", as a strategy for insuring that minorities have an equal chance to succeed, to "diversity", which, by contrast, is a moral description of the organization itself.

Affirmative action was conceived initially as a strategy that would give minorities and women an equal opportunity to be recruited and promoted. In this sense, affirmative action is an entirely pragmatic undertaking; it lives and dies on thoughtfully executed plans. It certainly has a moral component, but this component is grounded in the eminently practical idea of fairness (Adams, 1963).

By contrast, diversity is a moral category, a category for describing the ideal organization. As we know, the term "diversity" can mean either "diverse personalities", "diverse ethnic groups", or "diverse victim groups". The emotional weight of diversity derives from the last of these, so that diversity means that the organization is a mechanism for repairing past injustices. On the face of it, this might not seem to be such a great demand to make on organizations, but for the simple fact that the victim groups in question have fewer members who can compete for the most demanding jobs. This is, after all, one mark of their victim status: for example, their education is inadequate (Thernstrom & Thernstrom, 1999) Thus, the moral category of diversity sets up a tension between a commitment to the work of the organization and its moral standing. The problem, as we saw in Chapter One, is that the moral categorization in this case trumps the pragmatic; through political correctness, it subjects the pragmatist to the charge of being a bad person. Even bringing matters up that are important to the business makes one morally suspect. In other words, political correctness has organizational consequences. It becomes a part of the organization's decision-making process.

At a crucial meeting, Blair was promoted to the position of full-time staff reporter "with the consensus of a recruiting committee of roughly half a dozen people headed by Gerald M. Boyd, then a deputy managing editor, and the approval of Mr. Lelyveld". As we saw above, Landman, the metropolitan editor, opposed the promotion, but did not protest it because he endorsed the company's commitment to diversity (Barry, Barstow, Glater, Liptak, & Steinberg, 2003).

Yet, Landman was a conscientious editor, and knew full well the importance of the *Times*' maintenance of the paternal function. He had said in a staff e-mail: "Accuracy is all we have, It's what we are and what we sell" (*ibid.*). If we keep in mind that there is not supposed to be a conflict between the moral and the pragmatic grounds, it is worth asking what is the nature of the repression operating at this point that prevented Landman from registering an objection on those pragmatic grounds?

One way of understanding this repression is to imagine what Landman fantasized would happen if he shared his doubts. This may appear to be a somewhat reckless method for making inferences, but, on the other side, we suggest that in matters of race we all share a common and deeply held set of preoccupations so that we can enter into each other's minds. In this spirit, we suggest that Landman imagined that were he to call attention to Blair's incompetence he would be thought a racist. Why should this prospect disturb him, particularly if he believes it is not true? There is an irony here. Wrestling with the trade-off between excellence and diversity stimulates in people's mind the very racial idea that diversity programmes purport to eliminate. Making exceptions for blacks means that they cannot measure up. So, one reason Landman might fear being thought a racist is because at that moment he was, in fact, having thoughts that would, under the regime of political correctness, be regarded as racist.

But what prevented Landman from addressing this dilemma? Why couldn't he say, for example, "I know we might be touching on the sensitive issues of racism here, which I am perfectly prepared to address, but I think Blair is a danger to the *Times*." This imagined statement points to the problem. Landman cannot assume that people are perfectly prepared to address thoughts about race. The psychological strain imposed by political correctness is that the racial thoughts that are stimulated are simultaneously repressed. They are placed under a taboo.

The result of taboos is that people are unable to make meaning together on objective terms, even on issues that deeply concern them. This helps to explain why the editorial community at the *Times* could never come together to create a shared picture of Blair's frauds and their implications. The taboo undermined such meaning making. It made objective understanding, the paternal function, impossible.

The paternal function is the guardian of realistic thinking. When it is weakened, people are more likely to act on the basis of their wishes and fantasies rather than on the basis of the actual opportunities and threats they face. Thus, Landman says he thought that Blair seemed to be making the mistakes of a beginner and was still demonstrating great promise: "I thought he was going to make it" (Barry, Barstow, Glater, Liptak, & Steinberg, 2003). But, since

Landman had first-hand knowledge of Blair's performance and became increasingly alarmed by it soon after Blair's promotion, it appears that his hope for Blair did not arise from what he saw, but from what he wished to see.

The mental tension imposed by diversity is finally resolved when the black person can be thought of as a victim. This achieves three objectives; the black person's poor performance can now be acknowledged—they perform poorly *because* they have been victimized. The black person need not be held accountable for his or her actions, and, therefore, the white person need not be held accountable for failing to hold the black person accountable. This landscape of irresponsibility is another reason why Blair was never fired.

Organization and environment

The last level we will discuss involves the relationship between the organization, seen as a whole, and its environment. Within Oedipal psychology, this relationship is seen as a pattern of transactions, in which the organization produces something that the environment values, for which the environment supports the organization. These are objective relationships. As we saw earlier, the *Times* has a special relationship within them by being, in its paternal function, an important guarantor of objectivity, and, hence, a bulwark of the understanding that makes our society possible. This, however, is within the Oedipal framework. Throughout this chapter, though, we have argued that a shift is taking place towards an anti-Oedipal orientation, in which the *Times* comes to function, not as a father, but as a mother, loving those who have been deprived of love in the past and hating the father who has been the cause of that deprivation.

At the organization–environment level of analysis, one would look for this transformation in the work that the organization does; in the nature of its product. A shift from the paternal to the maternal would be represented by a shift in the *Times'* reporting from the representation of objective facts to advocacy. What is more, the advocacy would involve support for those seen as downtrodden and vituperation against the paternal function, against the father whose claim that there is an objective structure is seen as itself an agency for his oppression. Charges that such a shift has taken place have certainly been made, not only against the *Times*, but against much of the mainstream media. Such charges have been denied by people speaking for the media. For example:

> Our greatest accomplishment as a profession is the development since World War II of a news reporting craft that is truly non-partisan, and nonideological, and that strives to be independent of undue commercial or governmental influence. . . . It is that legacy we must protect with our diligent stewardship. To do so means we must be aware of the energetic effort that is now underway to convince our readers that we are ideologues. It is an exercise of, in disinformation, of alarming proportions. This attempt to convince the audience of the world's most ideology-free newspapers that they're being subjected to agenda-driven news reflecting a liberal bias. I don't believe our viewers and readers will be, in the long-run, misled by those who advocate biased journalism. [*New York Times* Executive Editor Howell Raines accepting the "George Beveridge Editor of the Year Award" at a National Press Foundation dinner shown live on C-SPAN2, February 20 2003, cited in Groseclose & Milyo, 2005]

However, validating or invalidating that charge is within the capacity of social science. In fact, such a study was undertaken by Groseclose and Milyo (2005). They examined the citation patterns in media news stories of various politically-orientated think tanks. They compared these with the citation patterns of various members of congress, whose location on the liberal–conservative dimension had been estimated by the Americans for Democratic Action. This allowed them to estimate ADA ratings for the various news outlets. They report:

> Our results show a strong liberal bias: all of the news outlets we examine, except *Fox News' Special Report* and the *Washington Times*, received scores to the left of the average member of Congress. Consistent with claims made by conservative critics, *CBS Evening News* and the *New York Times* received scores far to the left of center . . . All of our findings refer strictly to *news* content; that is, we exclude editorials, letters, and the like. [p. 1191]

In fact, "The *New York Times* is slightly more than twice as far from the center as [*Fox News*] *Special Report*" (*ibid.*, p. 1222)

To be sure, this is only one study, but our purposes do not require its conclusive verification. For one thing, the liberal–conservative dimension explored in the study is not the same thing as the distinction between the Oedipal and the anti-Oedipal, though the two are, no doubt, related. More importantly, our claim is not that the *Times* is monolithically one-sided. It is rather that the *Times* is the site of a contestation between the Oedipal and the anti-Oedipal, with the suggestion that the paper leans in the latter direction.

Conclusion

One of our concerns here has been to argue that the use of psychoanalytic theory, by focusing on meaning, provides a means for understanding society at any level. The links between behaviours, for example, Landman's reluctance to speak, Sulzberger's attack on Frankel at the executive retreat, Raines' speech at the National Association of Black Journalists, and Blair's sabotage, are connected not by a series of input–output relationships, but by their shared relationship to a single meaning The events do not stand in a relationship of cause and effect to each other, but, rather, in relationship to a shared symbolic context. Meaning itself is by definition immaterial; it has neither length, weight, nor colour. Rather, it has presence only in the mind. But, since minds can share meaning, the condition for co-ordinated action across many levels is established.

If this is so, the transformation at the *New York Times* has an important implication for American society in general. As we have said, the *New York Times* has a special place in the USA; it is not just an organization, but an institution, almost a structural element. The change of meaning we have seen, therefore, must be seen as being, at the same time, a shift in meaning within American society as a whole.

CHAPTER THREE

Religion against itself:
psychodynamics of some peculiar television commercials produced by the United Church of Christ

On 28 March 2006, the *San Francisco Chronicle* reported that the major TV networks had rejected an advertisement by the United Church of Christ, saying it violated their rules against controversial or religious advertising. The article, by Wyatt Buchanan, a *Chronicle* staff writer, says:

> The 30-second commercial for the United Church of Christ will begin airing on cable networks and Spanish-language stations next week. The ad, called "Ejector," shows a gay couple, a single mother, a disabled man and others flying out of their pews as a wrinkled hand pushes a red button. Text on the screen reads, "God doesn't reject people. Neither do we," and a voiceover says, "The United Church of Christ. No matter who you are or where you are on life's journey, you're welcome here." The church tried to run a similar ad in December 2004 in which bouncers outside a church stopped gay couples, racial minorities and others from entering. The networks also rejected that ad.

Both of the advertisements, which are available on the UCC website at http://www.ucc.org/god-is-still-speaking/televison-ads.html, are well produced and slick, and end with images of happy and diverse groups of people, evidently representing what the UCC has to offer. In both commercials, the familiar villains of political correctness have their places. In addition to the wrinkled hand, which is white and male, a stereotypic white middle-class family represents the membership of the church that excludes others. It appears to be their discomfort that provides the motivational basis for the ejections. They are not present among the happy and diverse people with whom the commercials end.

Blogger and political psychologist John Ray (2006), commenting on the article, said:

> A Leftist church (probably with a minute membership) was ostensibly trying to advertise itself but did so only by misrepresenting the great majority of Christian churches. No follower of Christ rejects anyone from Christian services—any more than Christ rejected lost sheep—but some churches will endeavour to point the way to more biblical standards of behaviour. Deceptive advertising is rightly banned and this ad was grossly deceptive and defamatory.

Doing a fast check through Wikipedia, I found out that, on one thing, Ray is wrong. The United Church of Christ cannot be said to have a minute membership. They say this about it:

> The United Church of Christ (UCC) is a mainline Protestant Christian denomination in the United States, generally considered within the Reformed tradition, and formed in 1957 by the merger of two denominations, the Evangelical and Reformed Church and the Congregational Christian Churches. Currently, the United Church of Christ has approximately 1.3 million members and is composed of approximately 5,750 local congregations.

On another matter, Ray is certainly correct. The advertisements are defining the UCC as a church that differs from the others in that it does not reject people such as gays. This definition only makes sense if it believes that such rejection is the norm among Christian churches. (Of course, the advertisements are not intended to be taken literally; their meaning is metaphorical. The question is what the metaphor represents. I assume, and I think we always do, that the metaphor itself is the best symbolic representation of the meaning of the metaphor. For our analysis, we need only to stipulate that we are analysing the commercials as metaphors and not as literal claims.) And, in fact, on its website it says, ". . . the ad acknowledges the rejection that many have experienced from organized religion".

This is what struck my attention. Here we have a charge of discrimination against an institution, mainstream Christianity, which, in my experience, is just as politically correct, and makes as much of a fetish of diversity, as any institution in American society. There was, it seemed to me, an antagonism in the charge that was not rooted in a realistic appraisal of what it was directed against. This suggests that the antagonism was not a response to something unacceptable in the outside world, but, rather, that its cause was endogenous. Thus, it seemed to me to be an instance whose exploration might reveal something about the nature of political correctness, where one frequently finds such inappropriate affects, in the sense of their being disproportionate to their presumed causes.

Placing the matter in context, Ray observes that Christian churches, followers of one who famously gathered social rejects around him, do not, as a general rule, reject people from services. On the contrary, in a manner that almost anyone would regard as definitional, Christians believe that Christ, through his sacrifice, offers us redemption from sin, and that it is one of the main functions of the Christian church to extend that offer of redemption. The result is that Christians characteristically deal with those they regard as sinners by offering salvation; attempting to bring the individuals into the fold, not by expelling them.

To be sure, there are matters that some would not consider sinful and others would. They might well feel themselves rejected. But that will always be so, as long as one holds that anything is sinful. But that there is sin is the very premise of Christianity. Jesus did not die on the cross to abolish the category of sin; he died to redeem us from it. And if Christians do not reject sin, even though they welcome the sinner as a person with a redeemable soul, it is hard to say how they can possibly be Christians.

Yet, the idea of Christians turning sinners away from services, absurd as it is, stands as nothing against the idea of Christians rejecting the disabled from services. The idea that followers of Christ, who largely ground their faith in the belief that Jesus worked miracles in healing the sick, would reject disabled people from services because they are disabled is more than absurd; it is bizarre.

The advertisements, that is to say, do not make a great deal of sense in their own right. That suggests that the way to understand them is not in their own right, but as the expression of irrational forces.

The purpose of the analysis

We can begin by focusing on a set of questions raised by the irrationality of the ads. First, what kind of attitude can it be that UCC believes other Christians have? Second, what is going on in the mind of the UCC, or rather of the UCC elite, that leads them to have the idea they have about other Christians? (When I speak here about the mind of UCC, I mean the mind of the UCC elite; those members who have the power to define the activities of the UCC, and who have defined it in terms of a certain outlook. It is the outlook that this elite share, together with the psychological processes that leads them to have this outlook, which is of interest to me. I do not mean the attitudes of ordinary UCC members, or, for that matter, the attitudes of the ordinary members of any of the mainline denominations. These are often strikingly different from those of the elite, a fact that has led to great conflict within the churches. For example, the elite of the Presbyterian church, speaking in the name of the church, passed a resolution supporting economic divestiture from Israel and condemning its security barrier. Shortly thereafter, a general meeting of church members voted, with a 95% majority, to rescind that resolution.) They certainly did not get that idea about other Christians from reality, since in reality other Christians do not have it. So where did they get it? Third, these advertisements are clearly acts of aggression. In the culture of political correctness, they are serious moral indictments of "organized religion". In the absence of a real basis for the charge, they must be based on an impulse to aggression that is within the mind of the UCC itself. What is the root of that impulse to aggression? Finally, how can it be that, quite contrary to fact, they believe it is ubiquitous?

The answer I will propose provides a key to all of these questions. It is that the attitudes that the UCC attributes to the minds of other Christians are not in other Christians, at least no more than they are in the mind of UCC members. UCC believes they are in the minds of other Christians because it has projected them there. It projected them there because it could not stand these attitudes being in themselves. By projecting them outside, UCC seemed to solve two problems. It could get rid of the unacceptable ideas and it could give them a locus outside themselves, which they could find unacceptable, and, in that way, maintain their hatred of the ideas. That is the root of the impulse to aggression. The reason they find these ideas ubiquitous is that they are everywhere they are, or imagine themselves to be, for the simple reason that UCC brings them along. What we are seeing here is the externalization of an internal conflict. It is not a conflict between UCC and other Christians, but within the mind of UCC itself.

But what are these ideas, and why are they so unacceptable? For an answer to that, we need to continue our analysis of the psychology of political correctness.

As we have seen, political correctness is based upon identification with the primitive image of an omnipotent, perfectly loving mother that we all carry with us in the deepest layers of our psyche. The infant is narcissistic; it experiences itself as being the centre of a loving world. The primitive mother personifies that loving world, and, hence, is part of the narcissism of the child. She is the infant's fantasy of mother, not a real mother, but she is eminently available for identification.

The appeal of such identification, in terms of the power and the sense of one's goodness and boundless love, is clear enough. However, it will pose problems for our engagement with reality, both external and internal.

The problem regarding external reality is what to do about our experience with aspects of the world that are not loving. As we know, the objective reality of the world is not built around us, and does not care about us. This objective, indifferent reality is personified in the father, and we respond to him with rage. Ordinarily, this rage is overcome by an internalization of the father, and the reality he represents. The formula for life, then, is to become like the father, accepting and living up to one's obligations in the world, and then you can have the mother, which is to say the world will revolve around you with love. We have referred to this set of dynamics as *Oedipal psychology*.

As we have seen, the solution that underlies political correctness is quite a different one. In this psychology, we deny the objective character of reality. Mother's omnipotence, her capacity to make our lives perfect just by her presence, would take care of us entirely, if her love had not been stolen by the father, who is seen here as an imposter. He has taken mother by force and subterfuge and stolen her love and beneficence from us.

The world is not indifferent to us. If it were not for him, the fantasy continues, the world would be a loving place, as it was when were infants in our mother's arms. Hence, the father represents the unloving aspects of the world. Our response to these aspects is to hate them, in the form of the father. Hating him, trying to expel him, and loving those from whom he has stolen mother's love, give rise to the very different approach to the world that I call anti-Oedipal psychology.

The problem regarding internal reality is what to do with parts of *ourselves* that are not loving.

The image of the primordial mother amounts to a deity. Our identification with this divinity requires that we have these perfect capacities ourselves. Being human, however, we never do. Our very humanity results in qualities that do not fit with a loving God. What are we going to do with these?

The point is that the ideology of inclusion is patently a maternal expression. If we take it as an absolute, these non-loving aspects become problematic for ourselves as well.

There are a number of such qualities. For one thing, as we have seen, there is recognition in our encounter with the father of our own incapacity and weakness. At the deepest level, the father, representing objective reality, bring us the news that we are human beings and, therefore, mortal. Within our identification with the primordial mother, these do not fit with our belief in our omnipotence. As we know, in the face of these experiences, we respond to him with rage and hatred. This problem has an internal aspect, because rage and hatred are not feelings that fit within the loving goodness of mother, either.

Another set of problems arises from the fact that, given the state of fusion, identification with the mother is also identification with her loved children. We cannot tolerate life being less than perfectly loving for any of these children, since that also undermines the omnipotence of mother's love. That, again, is the occasion of rage and hatred, and there we are with the same problem.

But there is another problem, which is perhaps the most threatening of all. It is that, in truth, we do not really love these children, either, or, at least, not in the way the primitive mother is supposed to love them. Remember, the premise here is narcissism. Identification with the children works both ways. Their narcissism is also our own narcissism. We can love them in so far as we can identify with them, but in so far as they are not ourselves, they are competitors and threats; their very existence as others demands love and attention that should be coming to us. Hence, we feel rage and resentment towards them, and these do not fit at all.

None of these feelings can be tolerated, let alone all of them. But what are we to do with them?

One possible resolution is to combine our internal problems with our external ones. If the perfect mother is the guarantor of everything good, then the father, who has taken the mother from us, is the cause of everything that is bad. This means that every intolerable feeling that we have can be consolidated and located in the father, or at least projected into him as their cause, and attacked there.

Thus, "organized religion", in so far as it is imagined as the rejecting church, may be seen as the representation of oppressive external reality and also as a repository created for the purpose of receiving the projection of intolerable feelings.

Thus, by adopting its maternal identification, the UCC was also defining itself as the father's antagonist. Given the grandiose premise, offering love, by itself, could not constitute a sufficient way of being; it had to be accompanied by a rejection of the father. These are two sides of the same coin. That is the complex dynamic that led to the creation of those peculiar commercials. And it is in the UCC commercials because it has come to be the central dynamic of the UCC. In large measure, it defines religion for them.

Two forms of Christianity

For psychoanalytic purposes, we may think of the ultimate object of religion as being the return to fusion with the primitive mother, which Freud (1914c, 1921c, 1923b) calls the ego ideal. As we have seen, though, there are two routes to the attainment of the ego ideal, which we have called the Oedipal and the anti-Oedipal. These give rise to two different conceptions of the nature of the church, which we may call the biparental and the maternal.

A church that takes an exclusively maternal orientation will be fundamentally different from a church that takes a biparental orientation. The promise of the biparental church, operating within the Oedipal dynamic, is, as we know, that if we become like the father, taking on and living up to the obligations in the father's understanding of reality, we can return to the state of fusion with the mother. In other words, if we fulfil the demands that God has made through religion, we can attain salvation and come home to God. At the same time, it also functions to explain why we have not attained the ego ideal; we have not entirely fulfilled those demands. In Christian terms, we remain sinners.

The maternal church, by contrast, operating in anti-Oedipal psychology, does not require living up to these demands; it abolishes the requirement of becoming like the father. Instead, its programme calls for reorientating our lives to be against the father. In so doing, it dissolves our separation from the ego ideal. It is now to be found within ourselves, if we can get rid of the father's intrusion. It offers us the ego ideal on the basis of inclusion in the body of the church, which, in both Oedipal and anti-Oedipal psychology, is a maternal element. However, inclusion on the basis of who we are means that there is nothing separating us from the attainment of God; we are already one with God. Hence, we must love as God loves.

This is quite an order. The problem is that our emotions are not under our control. We may experience God's love, Christians say, but when we do, it is a result of God's grace, and God is not under our control. Being only human, we cannot fulfil the emotional demands of perfect love.

What we can see in the commercials, explicitly in the group scenes at the end of the commercials, is identification with the mother; the UCC redefine their function in terms of maternal love. They will love each of us exactly as we are, and will make us feel perfectly loved in that way. This means that it has made demands upon itself and its members that they cannot fulfil.

Human limitations on the capacity to love and the limitations reality imposes on the efficacy of love keep us from the capacity for such fulfilment. But the maternal identification means that these limitations are not acceptable; hence, they have been projected out. "Organized religion", in so far as it is imagined as the rejecting church, is the repository for those projections. The offering of love had to be accompanied by hatred of organized religion, experienced in this way.

Organized religion, then, in the mind of the UCC is religion as organized by the hated father, in this case represented by the wrinkled hand, and by the person from whom the bouncers receive their orders. Take away the father and the members of the church will be as happy, comfortable, and universally loving as the diverse folks in the group scenes that end the UCC commercials. Indeed, given how wonderful this alternative is, the hatred and contempt for the father is further explained.

The point here is that hatred and rejection of the father, and hence of organized religion, is part of the essential makeup of the maternal church. This is obviously quite a significant redefinition of the nature of the church and religion, and we can see it taking place all through mainline American Protestantism.

The biparental church and the mother church

Consider an article in *First Things* magazine by Philip Turner (2005), the former Dean of the Berkeley Divinity School at Yale, and currently Vice President of the Anglican Communion Institute. His thought here is directed specifically at his own church, the Episcopal, but he means it to apply to all of mainline Protestantism within the USA, which would include the UCC.

Turner begins by reporting that after serving ten years as a missionary in Uganda, he returned to the USA to attend graduate school in Christian Ethics at Princeton. Subsequent to that, he took a job at the Episcopal Theological Seminary of the Southwest. This is what he reports:

Full of excitement, I listened to my first student sermon—only to be taken aback by its vacuity. The student began with the wonderful question, "What is the Christian Gospel?" But his answer, through the course of an entire sermon, was merely: "God is love. God loves us. We, therefore, ought to love one another." I waited in vain for some word about the saving power of Christ's cross or the declaration of God's victory in Christ's resurrection. I waited in vain for a promise of the Holy Spirit. I waited in vain also for an admonition to wait patiently and faithfully for the Lord's return. I waited in vain for a call to repentance and amendment of life in accord with the pattern of Christ's life.

This was quite different from what his ten years in Uganda would have led him to expect, and it was no aberration:

I have heard the same sermon preached from pulpit after pulpit by experienced priests. The Episcopal sermon, at its most fulsome, begins with a statement to the effect that the incarnation is to be understood as merely a manifestation of divine love. From this starting point, several conclusions are drawn. The first is that God is love pure and simple. Thus, one is to see in Christ's death no judgment upon the human condition. Rather, one is to see an affirmation of creation and the persons we are. The life and death of Jesus reveal the fact that God accepts and affirms us.

From this revelation, we can draw a further conclusion: God wants us to love one another, and such love requires of us both acceptance and affirmation of the other. [*ibid.*]

In other words, God is love and makes no demands on us. The church simply follows this model. This is what I am calling the mother church.

The mother church abandons its connection to its own doctrine, as it has come from the past and as it has been reinterpreted through learned and authoritative theological discussion. The word of God comes to be brought forward though spontaneity, within the overall frame of God's inclusiveness, guaranteed and validated by mother's love, and unconstrained by the necessity of linkage to tradition. In other words, the church speaks with the voice of God and what it does is an expression of divinity: ". . . changes in belief and practice within the church are not made after prolonged investigation and theological debate. Rather, they are made by 'prophetic actions' that give expression to the doctrine of radical inclusion" (*ibid.*).

Turner continues:

> Such actions have become common partly because they carry no
> cost. Since the struggle over the ordination of women, the Episcopal
> Church's House of Bishops has given up any attempt to act as a
> unified body or to discipline its membership.
>
> Certain justifications are commonly named for such failure of disci-
> pline. The first is the claim of the prophet's mantle by the innova-
> tors—often quickly followed by an assertion that the Holy Spirit
> Itself is doing this new thing, which need have no perceivable link
> to the past practice of the church. [*ibid.*]

The church as mother accepts us exactly as we are, makes no
demands and imposes no standards, apart from the embrace of
inclusiveness itself. For Turner, this represents the loss of what
makes Christianity Christianity; the Christian church, he says elsewhere (2003), is transformed into a simulacrum—an image of a
church. Our perspective leads us to see within it the rejection of the
Church as father, as he is represented in the demands made by
the Church:

> In a theology dominated by radical inclusion, terms such as "faith,"
> "justification," "repentance," and "holiness of life" seem to belong
> to an antique vocabulary that must be outgrown or reinterpreted.
> So also does the notion that the Church is a community elected by
> God for the particular purpose of bearing witness to the saving
> event of Christ's life, death, and resurrection.
>
> It is this witness that defines the great tradition of the Church, but
> a theology of radical inclusion must trim such robust belief. To be
> true to itself, it can find room for only one sort of witness: inclusion
> of the previously excluded. God has already included everybody,
> and now we ought to do the same. Salvation cannot be the issue.
> The theology of radical inclusion, as preached and practised within
> the Episcopal Church, must define the central issue as moral rather
> than religious, since exclusion is, in the end, a moral issue even for
> God.
>
> We must say this clearly: the Episcopal Church's current working
> theology depends upon the obliteration of God's difficult, redemp-
> tive love in the name of a new revelation. The message, even when
> it comes from the mouths of its more sophisticated exponents,
> amounts to inclusion without qualification. [*ibid.*]

Vicissitudes of the mother church

These dynamics are represented in the most striking form that the mother church has taken: the worship of the mother, and, by extension, the female, who, therefore, becomes elevated to the status of a goddess. When this happens, a more explicit expression of the maternal emotions involved comes to be on display, in a form that defines them in opposition to the demands made by traditional religion.

A classic example of this was a conference held in Minneapolis, November 4–7 1993. The conference was called "To re-imagine what belief in God and life together in community means from a Christian–feminist perspective". It was conceived by the Women's Ministry Unit of the Presbyterian Church (PCUSA), which contributed $66,000 and had twenty-four of their national staff there. Some 2,200 delegates attended, almost all of them lay-women and clergy from various Christian denominations, including 405 Presbyterians (PCUSA), 391 United Methodists, 313 Lutherans (ELCA), 234 Roman Catholics, and 144 from the United Church of Christ (Branch, 1994).

The following is from an article in *Christian Century* (1994):

> A defining point of the conference, according to some of its critics, was the use of the name Sophia, or "Divine Wisdom" personified in the Book of Proverbs, as a feminine name for God. Organizers developed elaborate worship rituals using feminine imagery, including that of Sophia.

The article goes on to list a number of other conference events that have caused controversy:

- an unscheduled gathering of about 100 lesbians on the dais, followed by a standing ovation from the audience;

- a panel on Jesus, in which Union Theological Seminary professor Delores Williams was quoted as saying, "I don't think we need folks hanging on crosses and blood dripping and weird stuff . . . we just need to listen to the God within.";

- a prayer offered to "earth maker Mauna, our creator," led by Melanie Morrison, cofounder of Christian Lesbians Out Together;

- a closing worship service featuring a ritual of milk and honey rather than the traditional bread and wine and including the words: "Our Sweet Sophia, we are women in your image. With the nectar between our thighs, we invite a lover; we birth a child; with our warm body fluids we remind the world of its pleasures and sensations . . ." [*ibid.*]

Not surprisingly, the conference came in for criticism from more traditional Christians. For example:

The whole Conference applauded heresy and celebrated blasphemy. Some of the statements were in extremely poor taste. For example, speaker Delores Williams referred to the biblical account of the conception of Jesus by saying that "the Holy Spirit mounted Mary." But even more appalling than the poor-taste-statement was the applause and laughter which followed.

Many basic doctrines essential to the Christian faith were repudiated at Minneapolis, often in an atmosphere of disrespect. These include the doctrine of God, the deity of Christ, His atoning death, the sinfulness of humanity, the Genesis account of creation, the authority of Scriptures, and the biblical understanding of human sexuality.

The entire Conference was an assault on the Gospel and a trampling under foot of key tenets of the Christian faith. The new religion promoted at the Re-imagining Conference soundly rejected the incarnation of Jesus, as well as His atonement on the Cross. The reporter in the Minneapolis *Star Tribune* said that the conference leaders were "re-shaping the Christian understanding of [the] foundations of theology." Participants and speakers alike angrily denounced the Christian church, charging that its teachings about Jesus Christ constitute the chief source of women's oppression, human violence, racism, sexism, classism, and the abuse of the earth. [Editorial, BRF Witness, 1994]

Interestingly, but also not surprisingly, from our standpoint, the response to this criticism saw it as coming from men's need to control women. For example, Patricia Rumer, general director of the group Church Women United, said that: "much of the criticism is coming from men who fear that women are gaining too much power: men need to silence this kind of thing in order to be in control." And:

Kathleen Clark, a laywoman with the UMC's Board of Global Ministries, said . . . "I was enthralled with the opportunity . . . to be a part of Re-Imagining, of expanding the concept of who we are as Christian people" . . . She expressed outrage at the backlash from more traditionally minded Christians. "What [critics] are saying is that women can't get together and talk and tell stories without their approval." [*Christian Century*, 1994]

But this criticism was based on nothing but traditional Christianity and its Gospel; so the implication is that traditional Christianity and the Gospel are attempts by men, the father, to control women. Without that, under the aegis of liberated women, the world would become a place represented and created by the free flow of imagination and desire, immune to the imposition of constraint. For traditional Christians, this dissolves Christianity altogether, leaving nothing but paganism:

Under the guise of Christian freedom, sin and spirituality are ritually wedded. At the *Re-Imagining Conference,* one of the speakers held up an apple, bit into it, and then with cheers from the audience asked, "What taboo have you broken today?" The taboo was the warning against apostasy found over again in the Scriptures. Their sacramental sacrilegious bite ingested the forbidden fruit of paganism, the worship of the creature rather than the Creator. [*CEP Equip*, 1997]

In Turner's terms, the mother church here is engaged in the project of obliterating Christianity. This project of obliteration is what we see in the commercials of the UCC.

Of interest to our analysis, though, is that the UCC project was unconscious. The conscious intention was rather different. In order to see this, we need to get a sense of the environment in which the church found itself, since consciously the church conceived of the commercials as a marketing strategy for coping with reality as it understood it.

The marketing strategy

The advertisements were part of a programme called The Stillspeaking Initiative (TSI). Its meaning is that God is still speaking, so we should pay attention to what He is saying now, rather than restrict ourselves to what He said in the past. The brainchild of a former marketing executive named Ron Buford, the project's conscious purpose was laid out in a series of annual reports put out by the UCC and available on their website.

We will turn to the specific rationale for the advertisements in a moment, but first of all we must give the matter a bit of context.

As I said above, UCC membership is by no means minute; however, it is shrinking. Having begun with 2.4 million members, it lost over 40% during the following fifty years. This was in keeping with the other mainline Protestant churches of the USA. (By "mainline", I mean the following churches: the American Baptist Churches, USA; the Christian Church [Disciples of Christ]; the Episcopal Church; the Evangelical Lutheran Church in America; the Presbyterian Church [USA]; the United Church of Christ; the United Methodist Church.) In 1960, mainline church membership stood at over 29 million. By 2000 this number had fallen to 22 million—a 21% drop. Some mainline denominations have suffered even greater membership losses: the Disciples of Christ, 55%, the Episcopal Church, 33%, in addition to the 39% drop of the UCC during this period.

This drop in membership needs to be contrasted with an overall increase in church membership within the USA during the same period. We will discuss the causes of this later on. For the present, note that during the same 1960 to 2000 period, the following changes took place in other, non-mainline denominations (Table 1).

Perhaps even worse from an organizational point of view was that donations from member congregations to the national church had declined even more substantially. The reasons for these declines are complex, and we shall return to them shortly. For

Table 1. Changes in church membership in the USA between 1960 and 2000.

Denomination	1960	2000
Assemblies of God	508,602	2,577,560
Southern Baptist Convention	8,731,591	15,960,308
Roman Catholic Church	42,104,900	63,383,030

the present, our interest is not in the real reasons, but in the UCC perception of the reasons. In so far as that perception has been publicly avowed, it provides the conscious rationale for the programme as a marketing innovation. To get a handle on it, we turn to the UCC annual reports, which are available on the UCC website at http://www.ucc.org/ocwm/.

The line of thought and action that culminates in the advertisements begins in the annual report for 2003, which notes the situation regarding membership and finances, and then announces what it plans to do about it:

> This annual report reflects our denomination's accomplishments and highlights and, if we are honest, our setbacks and shortcomings. It also announces the initiation of the Still Speaking Initiative—a bold plan for church-wide renewal. In the days ahead, our churches will hear more about the "God is still speaking," national identity campaign, which portrays the story, image and ministry of the United Church of Christ, inviting the unchurched into our congregations.

The advertisements, then, will be part of a strategy to invite the unchurched into the UCC, as well as to increase contributions to support activities at the national level (referred to as the OCWM).

It is anticipated that this programme will place them "at odds with society . . . requiring resistance, daring and decisive action", as it did for their forebears:

> We often have been referred to as the "early" church, because we've been early in addressing the important issues facing our society and taking uncomfortable positions that sometimes go against cultural acceptability. Why? Because we love Jesus more than the lure of respectability.

Taking these positions meant being the first mainline church to take a public stand against slavery, and ordaining the first woman and the first gay person.

Thus, they are placing the action they are going to take in the same vein as social action initiatives they have undertaken in the past, and which they say have cost them some respectability.

They lay out the programme in this way:

These are tough times for the Church. Giving is down in mainline churches and, on Sunday mornings, most pews are filled with graying worshipers. A recent survey revealed that 87 percent of Americans feel that religion is important to their lives. Yet only 42 percent of Christians attend worship services on a regular basis. Even more startling—85 percent of mainline churches are in a state of membership decline.

If so many people feel that religion is important, why do so few attend church? There are several reasons: a large segment of our society has little or no church background; others feel that worship is boring and uninspiring; some maintain the church has lost its vision in society; others have had a negative personal experience in the church and feel unwelcome . . .

The Still Speaking Initiative . . . is in the initial stages of addressing the many challenges before us—spiritual, financial, and demographic. New television commercials will air in 2004 to let the unchurched know about the UCC's unique witness and welcome.
. . .

The 2004 annual report follows in this vein, and the programme becomes evident:

2004 began with a mad scramble. The decision had been made—full speed ahead with a strategic, five-year marketing plan to proclaim to the world that anyone could find a home in the United Church of Christ. The Stillspeaking Initiative was formally established as an independent, inter-covenantal department reporting to the Executive Council, and an advisory task group was created . . . [The shift in spelling from Still Speaking to Stillspeaking is in the original]

From this, it appears that the decision to launch the programme, with its advertisements, had been made. It was only after this that the advertising agency set up focus groups to find evidence. Not surprisingly, they did:

Everyone had a story stemming from personal rejection, disappointment, and the failure of the church to be there for them. . . . Participants were unanimous—the church needs to be a welcoming place that uplifts one's self-image and encourages individuals to be a vital member of the community. . . . The focus group leaders concluded that alienation was at the heart of these individuals' disaffection with the church. "Alienation is about real personal experiences and deep hurts that have caused people to turn away from the church. It is not about the rejection of God or spirituality. . . . Facilitators observed, "There appears to be a genuine opportunity to bring these people back because they are open to a welcoming church community and extended support system." The final report provided clear direction: "A positive, welcoming, come as you are message will reach the desired audience."

They describe the meaning of the commercial this way:

The 30-second TV commercial, "The Bouncer," has been hailed as a masterful piece of storytelling in the tradition of Jesus' parables. The burly bouncers are a metaphor for that which alienates people from the church. While no church actually has bouncers outside its doors, it's obvious to many (often through the painful experience of rejection) that they are held at arm's length. For whatever reason— age, ethnicity, disability, socio-economic status, sexual identity, whatever—these children of God, in search of a spiritual home, feel left out in the cold.

Along with the advertisement, UCC redesigned its website to focus on the advertisement and The Stillspeaking Initiative (TSI), which had its own website and its own logo.

The logo of the UCC is fairly conventional (Figure 1).

The symbol of the TSI is a comma, from a quote attributed to Gracie Allen: "Never place a period where God has placed a comma."

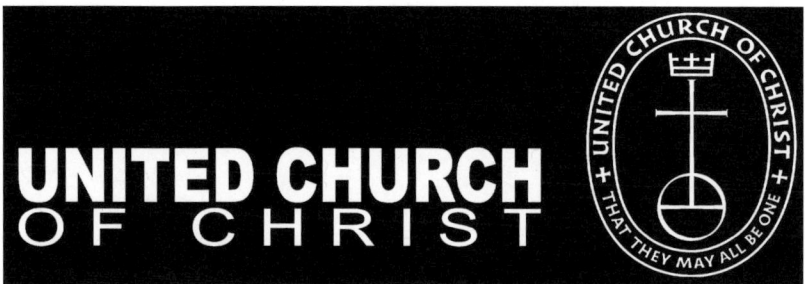

Figure 1.   Logo of the United Church of Christ.

The home page of the UCC website was rebuilt around that comma, which had a flash display with pictures of diverse, smiling people running through it. The text that goes with the comma is "God is still speaking".

In fact, the TSI crowded out the older image of the UCC. The logo of the UCC was small and below the main display. On many computers it would not show up in the initial screen, one would have to scroll down to find it, and there was no reason in the initial screen to suppose that one would find anything by scrolling down. Many of the links took one to the TSI website, from which it was not easy to get back. Though it did not say so, the search engine to find churches in one's area brought back only the minority of churches that had endorsed TSI. One needed to go elsewhere in the site to find a search engine that listed all UCC churches. On a professionally developed website, such a pattern does not occur through inadvertence.

At any rate, to hear UCC tell the story, they were on the verge of something big. According to them, part of the reason was that the commercials had been turned down by the networks:

> With the roll-out of the commercial on independent and cable stations, and the resulting denial by CBS, NBC and ABC to air the commercial, we received more publicity than we could have hoped for. During December, we posted 787,056 web visits (compared to 80,000 per month earlier in the year) and 137,103 visits to the "Find a UCC Church" option (there were 4,000 hits in November).
>
> Testimonies from people alienated by the church filled e-mail boxes at the national setting, and many stories of hope were shared on the special edition Yule Blog at ucc.org. Stories from pastors also flooded in, many about visitors checking out their churches . . .

Under the headline "Stillspeaking's 'bouncer' receives 'biggie' advertising award", the Church announced that

> The UCC's "bouncer" television commercial, which aired nationally in December 2004 and March 2005, has received one of the advertising industry's most significant honors.
>
> The Association of National Advertisers awarded the United Church of Christ with its 2005 Multicultural Excellence Award for its 30-second commercial that touted the denomination's insistence that "Jesus didn't turn people away. Neither do we".

But whatever awards and publicity were garnered by the advertisement, as far as its recruitment purpose was concerned, it was a flop. According to the 2006 yearbook of the National Council of Churches (NCC), membership dropped during 2004 by 2.38%, the largest decline of any church surveyed. To be sure, there was only one month in 2004 in which the effect of the commercial could have been felt, but a landslide had been expected. Worse, the NCC yearbook for 2006 revealed that membership in 2005 fell to 1,229,953, a drop of 3.3% from the previous year.

Although they were surely aware of these trends as they were developing, UCC was undeterred and pushed ahead with the second commercial, which was to be part of a campaign budgeted at 1.5 million dollars. "To change would be to back down. And the U.C.C. is not an institution that traditionally backs down," said Michael Jordan of Gotham, the UCC advertising agency.

Yet, reality still refused to shape up, and in the end it had its way. On 7 June 2006, the UCC announced that Ron Buford had resigned as head of TSI, effective from 30 June, and that he would take up a new role as "consultant with the Congregational Vitality Initiative (CVI) of the UCC's Local Church Ministries to assist trainers who will incorporate the best of The Stillspeaking Initiative into CVI" (Administrator, 2006).

(At this time, the TSI website, though removed from its dominant position, is still available from the UCC site, and still celebrates the joyfulness of the campaign.)

However, as this was going on, without fanfare, they added another commercial to their site. This one, which had been intended as a follow-on to the Bouncer commercial, but almost never aired, was called "Steeples". It began with a little girl reciting the nursery rhyme "Here is the church, here is the steeple, open the doors and see all the people." Then representatives of the groups that were rejected in the Bouncer commercial, including blacks, lesbians, Hispanics, and disabled people, appear sequentially to say "all the people". Finally, the same diverse group as in the Bouncer commercial, repeats "all the people" and there is the voice-over that says, "God accepts all the people, so do we. The United Church of Christ. No matter who you are or where you are on life's journey, you're welcome here."

The unconscious meaning of the commercials

Consciously, the campaign was surely intended to reverse the decline in membership. But the failure of the programme suggests that there were shortcomings in the reasoning behind it, which raises the possibility that there were serious irrational elements that helped to determine the way it developed. Irrationality is not difficult to find here.

For one thing, as I have noted above, the focus groups, which were presumably intended to objectively determine whether there was a desire that the UCC could fulfil, were formed only after the decision was made about the nature of those needs. They were formed, that is to say, not for exploration, but for confirmation.

For another thing, the church's celebration of the positive response the commercials were receiving was focused largely on enthusiasms they had no reason to relate to any interest in taking up what the church had to offer. For example, it is difficult to see how the marketing professionals who were impressed by the advertisement would have any affinity with the alienated and wounded people that the advertisements were presumably intended to reach. Similarly, taking the popularity of the UCC website as an index of success ignored the much more likely possibility that it had been due to curiosity about the motivation behind the unusual commercials, rather than an interest in what it had to offer as a church.

Finally, the church's continuance of this expensive campaign, in the face of its clear failure to meet its ostensible objectives, strongly suggests that its conscious objectives did not represent the totality of its meaning for the UCC. All of this gives us leave to look at anomalies in the commercials, with an eye towards discerning the difference between their conscious and unconscious meaning.

"A letter," says Jacques Lacan (1988), "always arrives at its destination." The failure of the advertising campaign makes it legitimate to question the motivation behind it, and to ask whether, at some level, it was intended for another purpose, and one that it actually achieved.

As we saw, the commercials were introduced with the prediction that they would garner social disapproval. With regard to motivation, this raises the question as to what there could be about "inviting the unchurched" that could be seen as the kind of ground-breaking progressive move that would do that. What did UCC have in mind that would be "risky", and would "embody resistance and daring?"

In fact, they did lose respectability. But the negative response of the networks was not about the inclusiveness, *but about the offensiveness of the advertisements themselves.* The disapproval they rightly anticipated was not to the content of the offering, but to their manner. This suggests that the meaning of the advertisements was not the offer of welcome.

The message of welcome, as such, was represented in the advertisements by the final images of happy, diverse groups of people. In fact, this was the full content of the "Steeples" advertisement, which was almost never aired and was actually accepted by the networks. The offer of welcome was obviously not what made the advertisements stand out. What gave the advertisements their characteristic identity was the accusation of a refusal of welcome on the part of "organized religion". What the advertisements offered is not so much a welcoming church as an aggressive church: a church that resists and attacks the oppression represented by other churches. This is the only element of the advertisements that they could possibly have had in mind when they prepared the ground for social disapproval. It was, of course, the antagonistic side that created the controversy and that was clearly responsible for the "edge" of which the UCC was so proud.

It was "organized religion" that was rejecting people, causing them to be alienated from religion, and doing this in sufficient numbers that these rejects could be energized by the advertisement into joining the UCC and rejuvenating it. It was this idea, combined with their placement of themselves in contrast to "organized religion" by offering what they called "extravagant welcome" that gave the advertisements their particular flavour and their edginess. This suggests that the ostensible recruitment objective was only one of the objectives. The other was the attack upon "organized religion".

As we saw at the beginning, though, the charge that organized religion was rejecting people, especially on the basis of disabilities, is absurd. UCC could not have obtained the idea from observation of organized religion in the world. What exactly was it that they saw themselves as attacking, and how did they get that idea?

Rejection in the mind of UCC

We can get insight into the mind of the UCC from a website they set up to garner stories in response to the ads: www.rejection-hurts.com This website, which has since been taken down, offered itself as "An online community where people can share their personal stories of how they felt unwanted or alienated by organized religion". The stories were prefaced with this:

> Have you or someone you know ever felt rejected by religion? Tell us your story here. Please refrain from mentioning specific denominations or churches in your story.

> We will regularly post some of the stories that have been submitted. We encourage you to visit this site often and pass it on to your family and friends.

I would like to note, at the outset, the evident conflation between feeling "unwanted or alienated by organized religion" and feeling "rejected by organized religion". Rejection, one would suppose, implies a positive, directed antagonism; not being wanted, however, is consistent with passive indifference. The conflation is an important one, and will tell us much about the mind of UCC.

Turning to the stories themselves, it must first be said that many describe events that it is hard to believe have been objectively reported, or that the full story has been told.

Our interest, though, is not in whether the stories were true; we cannot know that. What we can know, and what interests us, is the fact that UCC chose these stories to represent the kind of responses they thought validated their commercials. They tell us what the meaning of the commercials was to UCC, and therefore offer insight into the way the church saw itself.

The following themes emerge from the stories.

First, there was no recognition on the part of any of these story tellers that anything that they did was in any way responsible for the outcomes they experienced. These were all stories of egregious victimization at the hands of the rejecting church.

My favourite in this regard was the story called: *Mohawks Not Welcomed*:

> I am gothic and a christian [*sic*]. I happily attended a [non-UCC] church until I went on their youth camp. I was put into the communal sleeping area with the 13–17 year olds (I am 21), and the entire weekend I had people coming up to me asking if I wanted them to pray with me, just because I had a mohawk [this is a type of haircut, named after the Mohawk Indian tribe, in which the head is shaved, except for a narrow band of hair that runs from front to back] and wore thick black eyeliner. Their "meetings" were compulsary [*sic*] and they kept on encouraging people to come up to the front and get prayed over, to the point where they were threatening to point out individuals in the congregation. When I tried to leave the meeting, they said that I had to stay or they would send me home in a taxi (which would have cost about $150). After the camp was over, I never went back to that church again.

Consider here the way the writer takes the response to his Mohawk and eye-liner, which can have no function except to elicit a response, as illegitimate on the part of the church. There is no acceptance of responsibility for causing that response.

A second point is the failure to distinguish between indifference and rejection. For instance:

When a Church's "Helping" Only Hurts

> I was raised in a literalist church. In my mid-teens I was doubting, and discouraged by treatment from the other teens. After all the youth programs, adult classes, and every Sunday worship, a woman with whom I had long worshipped shook my hand during one service and asked if I was new because she'd never seen me. It shook my core that "godly people" would consider me so invisible. It was a signpost of that church's lacking. It was also the chisel-tap for years of suicidal depression . . . I am glad for the message and hospitality (and the seeking and partnering attitude) of the UCC, and the fair treatment I've received. If other churches feel a sting from its message, then they should do some soul-searching. (I already did—now it's their turn.)

In some cases, there is a failure to acknowledge the viability of any rules or demands. In some cases this concerns specific moral principles, such as rejection of homosexual behaviour, divorce, or sex outside of marriage. In some cases, it runs to a rejection of rules altogether:

Stipulations Not Required

I recently saw your commercial and I was shocked, I've been searching for many years to find some thing worth believeing [*sic*] in but every major relegion [*sic*] has every kind of stipulation imaginable (even though the bible says not to judge). Seeing that commercial gave hope to a very discouraged girl. And I pray that you truly stand for every thing you advertised. I'll be checking out you [*sic*] site.

Often, general moral rules are seen as personal affronts:

Twice Rejected

After 24 years in my church, I married a man of a different denomination, in his church. My church didn't seem to care about that, I was welcome. Three years later, we'd divorced due to his mistreatment of me and his abandonment of the marriage. Not long after, I was told that I could attend church, but I couldn't participate in communion because I'd married outside the faith and then divorced. I still attended, but sporadically. One Sunday, my mother convinced me to go to church with her. Everything was fine until the sermon. It was about the "signs of death in the church". According to the sermon, the worst was divorce and that those that divorce are going to hell. I was furious. I had done nothing wrong, and I was being told I was going to hell. I turned to my mother, told her I was leaving and would never again set foot in that church.

Fourth, there is in many stories a failure of the sense of proportion. Personal offences are generalized to the church, or small events are elevated to massive assaults, as was visible in the passage from "When a Church's 'Helping' Only Hurts", above, and which was followed later by:

In college, I was accosted by a teen girl whose church had sent her youth group to collar concert-goers and follow them to their cars arguing salvation, as if that would convince someone to instantly fall to the sidewalk and "become a new creature through Christ." I was appalled and insulted by their naively unquestioning insinuations—the only "new creature" I'd become was ignored and suicidal. I was so angry at her hubris I wanted to punch her.

Finally, while demands made upon the individual are denied and seen as affronts, demands made upon the church, even when unreasonable, are seen as entitlements. For instance, in the first story above, Mr Mohawk takes it as one of the church's affronts that "When I tried to leave the meeting, they said that I had to stay or they would send me home in a taxi (which would have cost about $150)." Now, the only way this makes sense is if we assume that Mr Mohawk wanted to be driven home, either in an individual's car or in the church bus, and that this must have been, given the taxi fare, quite a far distance. He is taking their perfectly reasonable refusal as personal abuse.

What stands out about these accounts in the first place, as I said above, is the denial of responsibility. No student of psychoanalysis will be surprised at such denial of responsibility, but we need to understand that we are looking at a Christian church here, and that one of the defining tenets of Christianity is the belief that we are all sinners. The acceptance of oneself as a sinner is acceptance of responsibility. By standing behind the moral validity of these stories, the UCC was accepting the denial of responsibility as a valid ground for membership in a Christian church and, in fact, validating the deflection of that responsibility on to the rejecting church itself.

Second, of equal importance, is that they are all expressions of resentment. They all represent personal grievances, typically petty, which are elevated to the point of high principle. The premise appears to be that the world is supposed to conform itself to our wishes and validate us just as we are. When it does not, that is taken as a moral failure on the part of the world. The magnitude of this moral failure is equal to the value we place upon ourselves, which is, essentially, infinite.

Third, the indifference of reality is denied. The cause of their unhappiness is personalized and seen as the expression of a malevolent will, which in most cases is specifically directed against them.

From what we have said before, we can see that a demand is being made upon the world to act as if it were the primitive mother. Fusion is taken to be the basis of their relationship with others. This represents the loss of the boundary between the self and what is not the self. When the world does not love them absolutely, the individuals feel violated and attacked. For a church to define itself as a place that will fulfil these individuals' wishes, providing a feeling of validation to all these individuals who feel as if they have been rejected, means that the church is offering itself in just that maternal way.

But here we see the aggression that, for humans, goes along with that maternal identification. The UCC is accepting these individuals as they are, but they are filled with resentment. The problems they have are entirely the fault of others. To accept them as they are is to identify with and validate their denial of responsibility and resentment. The UCC is not simply offering inclusion; it is taking their side in their hatred and rejection of the indifference of reality, accepting their interpretation that it is a malevolent force that is persecuting them. The church is joining them in blaming the world for their distress, specifically represented as "organized religion". From what we have said before, we can see this spectre as a manifestation of the father.

Denial of aggression

What goes along with this is a denial of aggression on the part of UCC. The advertisements are clearly accusations, aggressive acts, as the networks made plain in their rejections. For example:

> NBC did accept one of the church's ads, according NBC spokeswoman Shannon Jacobs, but the church has not asked it to run that ad. According to Jacobs, the church proposed two ads, NBC accepted one but rejected the other because it "violated our long-standing policy against accepting ads dealing with issues of public controversy." The controversy, said NBC, stemmed from the ad's suggestion that "other religions are not open to all people."

> Specifically, NBC said it rejected the advertisement not because it featured a homosexual couple, but "based solely on the fact that it suggests that gay couples, African Americans, Hispanics and people with disabilities are not welcome in some churches, which constitutes a controversial issue". [Eggerton, 2004]

However, the UCC denies any aggression, saying that they are just messages of inclusion. In their view, the advertisements were rejected because the "message of openness and welcome stated in the new UCC ad is 'too controversial'". This is from an e-mail sent out by the Justice and Witness Ministries (JWM) of the UCC:

> Once again, a new UCC commercial, which invites all people into the church, has been rejected by the networks, their affiliate cable stations, and Viacom. Every day, the networks air advertising laced with sexual innuendo, violence, materialism, and the politics of personal destruction, yet the message of openness and welcome stated in the new UCC ad is "too controversial" to be shown. While some stations are still airing our ad, many communities, particularly those without access to cable, will never see this ad.

If a spokesperson for CBS is to be believed, it appears that TSI director Buford went so far as to make up a conversation.

> Buford said CBS executives had told him the subject would be considered advocacy advertising until the inclusion of gays and lesbians is common at churches in the USA. But [CBS spokeswoman Shannon] Jacobs (a web search reveals that both CBS and NBC employ a Shannon Jacobs in corporate communications; whether this is the same Shannon Jacobs, I cannot say) challenged that statement. "That supposed exchange is simply fictitious," she said. [Buchanan, 2006]

We have no reason to doubt Buford's sincerity in his contrary recollection of the conversation. He is probably just remembering what went on in the only way that he could make sense of it, and then just filling in details that fit. The primitive mother, after all, is made out of love. There is no aggression in her, so therefore UCC always acts with love and nothing but love. The aggression is externalized on to those who refuse to accept and amplify the message of her love, and then seen as directed against her and her clientele.

This is the equivalent of what we said above about the validation of resentment. Others see aggression, because it is clearly there. The UCC misses the aggression because the aggression is part of what it means by love. That is why it sees only love and welcome on its part. But it loves and includes the resentment and transmits it in the form of the aggression in the advertisements.

Inevitably, the resentment has come to cover the networks' rejection of the advertisements on the basis of their aggression. UCC has been treated unjustly, they believe; their heart, in their mind, is pure. Still, the fit between them and the resentful individuals they welcome is manifest.

Marketing the mother church

Interestingly, it appears that, despite what UCC thought it found in its focus groups, it is the paternal church that appeals to parishioners, not the maternal. This is suggested by the rise in membership of more traditional denominations during the period of mainline decline, which we noted earlier and which is borne out by some specifically directed research.

One of the better studies of recent times was done by Johnson, Hoge, and Luidens (1993). Their study confirmed that many had left the mainline church and that, for the most part, this was due to the fact that religion had become low on their list of priorities. Of those who remained, the best single predictor of church participation turned out to be orthodox Christian belief, particularly the idea that a person can only be saved through Jesus. Among church members, they found support for the view that the mainline churches had lost support because they had become weak as religious bodies, offering a diversity of theological viewpoints, no compelling answer to questions concerning the meaning of life, no distinctive code of conduct, and no discipline for violating what there was of it. Strong religious bodies, doing the opposite, foster a high level of commitment that binds members to the group.

Similarly, within the mainline dominations themselves, in general, it was those with evangelic pastors that were doing well, while the others were not (Hamilton & McKinney, 2003).

In a word, the biparental church, with its paternal aspect strongly represented, grows stronger, while the mother church declines. We may add, on the basis of what we have said before, that in many cases weak maternal churches had become, to use Turner's term, simulacra; images of churches whose anti-Oedipal ideology was essentially political, not religious. It appears that those were the institutions that went into decline.

The story of the United Church of Christ

How could it be otherwise? For Christians, Christ offers salvation and the meaning of Christianity is to attain salvation. It is contained within the very idea of salvation that it is a matter of transcendental importance. Anyone who believes in salvation will, as a matter of logic, think of it that way. But it is inconsistent with the idea of its importance that it should come cheaply and without effort. If it were the sort of thing that could come easily, it would not have been necessary for Christ to die on the cross to bring it to us. Hence, for Christians, the only church that can be a valid Christian church is one that requires us to take a difficult path to our salvation. That difficult path is what is offered by traditional Christianity, the Christianity of the paternal element in the biparental church.

It is hard to see how a Christian could take seriously a "come as you are" church like that offered by the elite of the UCC. To be sure, it could be taken seriously as something else: as a political action group, for example. But here is where the logic of religious organization poses a terrible question for such churches: who needs them? Why would an individual committed to political action need to come to a church to do it? Why not cut out the middle-man and go directly to a political action organization?

One possible reason is that the church could be seen to provide a resource that could be mobilized for political purposes. The church, in other words, could be seen as ripe for co-option into a political programme by those to whom political action is most important. One can easily see, though, that, over time, the church used in this way would lose its appeal to those who came for other reasons. It would lose membership, and those who remained would resist the politics that they would see as an intrusion.

More than that, an elite that came to dominance in that church, for the purpose of using it as a political instrument, would have contempt and resentment for its more traditional membership. This contempt and resentment could easily express itself as moral repudiation, as we saw in the television commercials, as well as actions that would have the unconscious purpose of ejecting the church's own religiously orientated members, under the aspect of "organized religion". This antagonistic attitude helps to explain one further aspect that we have yet to fully engage, which is the UCC's stance on homosexuality.

Homosexuality

·The issue of homosexuality clearly has a special significance in the current situation of the UCC, as it has within the whole Christian movement. It seems clear that, when the Church adopted the theme of welcoming the rejected, homosexuals were high on the list of those who were being welcomed. In fact, the UCC encourages its churches to declare themselves Open and Affirming, in accordance with a resolution passed at the 1985 Synod (http://www.ucc.org/lgbt/ona.html). Resistance on the part of the membership, however, was evident in the fact that only about 400 congregations, out of about 6,000, adopted that designation.

Another resolution, passed at the 2005 Synod, which affirmed UCC support for Equal Marriage Rights, was clearly the occasion for a large increase in the number of people and congregations leaving the Church.

Obviously, the issue of homosexuality encapsulates the conflict between the maternal and paternal aspects of the church. This is not only in the sense that it is an assault against received religious doctrine, but because it redefines the basis of the relationship between the parents, turning the relationship of men and women from a bedrock of morality into a matter of taste, disconnected from anything else, and, hence, radically undermining the meaning of being a father.

What we can see from this is that the issue of homosexuality is part of a general anti-Oedipal political stance, part of its programme of political correctness. The religiously orientated churches objected to political correctness, but, arguably, up until the matter of homosexuality, they tolerated political pronouncements made by the national organization, since they had no real impact on the practices of the local churches. There was, in a sense, a division into spheres of influence. The issue of homosexuality blew that boundary apart by imposing the politics of the national elite on the practices of the local churches. (The case of the UCC is arguably a bit different than other mainline churches in this regard. It has a "congregational" polity that recognizes the autonomy of local churches. In the form of its resolutions, the national body is said to *speak to* the local churches, rather than to *speak for* them. But this is a formal distinction only. In fact, the national resolutions present the public face of the church, which the public applies to its members, whether they are legally bound or not, and to which they are naturally sensitive.)

The problem was that traditional Christianity rests on the Bible, whose condemnation of homosexual behaviour is clear. For instance: "Thou shalt not lie with mankind, as with womankind: it is abomination" (Leviticus 18: 22). And:

> For this cause God gave them up unto vile affections: for even their women did change the natural use into that which is against nature: And likewise also the men, leaving the natural use of the woman, burned in their lust one toward another; men with men working that which is unseemly, and receiving in themselves that recompense of their error which was meet. [Romans 1: 26–27]

To be sure, some commentators have reinterpreted such passages in ways that attempt to attenuate the conflict between Christianity and homosexuality (e.g., Boswell, 1981; see http://www.religioustolerance.org/hom_bibx.htm for a good overview). There cannot be a doubt, however, that traditional Christianity has seen a serious conflict here, and that is what is at issue for us.

The view I am taking must be contrasted with another view, which is that the Church found the issue of the exclusion of homosexuals so morally compelling that it adopted its positions, including the various resolutions and the Stillspeaking Initiative, as a way of satisfying this moral imperative, despite the negative responses it knew it would generate. On this view, the other categories of exclusion were added as a kind of camouflage, to generate additional moral authority in the face of the expected attack. This view would be consistent with the emotional heat that their programme generated, and it would certainly be consistent with the view they held of themselves as courageous.

But the politics of this matter lead me to reject this view. The point here is that the issue did not arise over homosexuals being members of the UCC; rather, the issue arose over *making the issue an issue*. By making public pronouncements, the UCC elite put the membership in the position of having to respond publicly on a matter that, in individual cases, could have been quietly and privately finessed, on the basis of their own dispositions and interpretations of religion. By making it into a public matter of principle, the Church elite cast many of its own members on a side where they would be subject to open moral derogation by their own church, and they certainly knew this would happen. In a word, the issue was not one of universal inclusion, but rather of forcing the exclusion of some, the traditional element, by forcing a choice over the inclusion of the others. It was another act of egregious aggression. Rather than accepting a fight because of a stand on an issue they thought was important, they made the issue important as a way of creating a fight.

This dynamic was clearly in evidence in the case of the ordination of a gay bishop by the US Episcopal Church. In this case, V. Eugene Robinson was consecrated in November 2003 as bishop for the State of New Hampshire, despite considerable opposition among Episcopalians in the USA and against the clear opposition of the worldwide Anglican movement, of which the Episcopal Church is part. A report by an Anglican Church Commission (Lambeth Commission on Communion, 2004) said the Episcopal Bishops

> acted in the full knowledge that very many people in the Anglican Communion could neither recognize nor receive the ministry as a bishop in the church of God of a person in an openly acknowledged same-gender union. ,

The Episcopal decision began a process that seems to be leading to the fracture of the worldwide Anglican Church, as the Episcopal bishops knew it would. But notice that the issue was not the inclusion of homosexuals; it was the promotion of a homosexual into the highest rank. There was no grievous moral wrong that cried out to be righted; the number of those consecrated as bishops is necessarily small, and there will always be multiple factors that need to be taken into consideration. It would not have been out of place if the bishops had considered that his elevation would alienate many from the Church. This was an issue that did not need to be made. In the case of Robinson, who left his wife for another man, one would have easily thought that the sin of fornication, or sex outside of marriage, would have been grounds to avoid confrontation, whatever other virtues he possessed, if there had been a will to do so. That the decision to promote him was made suggests that it was taken because of its promise to create alienation, not despite it.

Conclusion: the insupportability of being merely human

In the commercials, the actual rejection is done by the church's elite. But the commercials have been created by the church's elite. This apparent self-reference suggests that there may be a deeper level of analysis, and one on which it would be suitable to end.

In the commercials, it appears that those being rejected are the ones who make church members uncomfortable. I suggest that, at a deeper level, something else is going on. It is not only those who cause the discomfort that are being rejected, but the discomfort is also being rejected. The rejectees are functioning as classic scapegoats; they are taking the sins of the group along with them. That is their function: they have the purpose of maintaining the image of the group as the ego ideal by representing its shameful elements, which are then rejected.

But whose discomfort is it that is being rejected? I suggest that it is the discomfort of the church's elite. They are, after all, the elite of a Christian church, a religion whose foundational premise is that we are all sinners. But as we have seen, this Church elite has identified itself with God, who, of course, has no sin. This poses a real problem for them.

Ordinary Christians may be able to maintain an image of themselves as sinners; this means that they can acknowledge and own their own discomfort. Therefore, their discomfort does not pose a problem for the church, and cannot be the psychological ground of the rejection. We can see this most clearly in the element of the commercials that appears to be most odd, which is the rejection of the disabled. As we saw, there cannot be a serious claim that a Christian church would turn somebody away because the person cannot walk. But there is certainly a basis for saying that people, probably most people, feel discomfort in the presence of a person who has lost the use of his legs. They remind us of the short distance between our own health and our own potential disability; indeed, our own death. We do not want to know about this, and, therefore, are uncomfortable in the presence of someone who brings it to our mind.

But this is as likely to be true of the church elite as of anyone else, and, indeed, more so, precisely since they cannot acknowledge their discomfort. Hence, there is no ground for saying that the rejection is less about the elite than it is about anybody else. But their discomfort is absolutely intolerable to them. Something must be done with it.

We began this analysis with the question: who is the rejecting church, and what are they rejecting? The answer is that the rejecting church is the elite of the UCC, and they are rejecting themselves. They are both rejecter and rejected.

This is what I call religion against itself.

Conclusion

To the extent that the dynamics in operation at UCC represent something at the core of political correctness, that provides us with a certain insight. It is that the anger one often sees in PC, and which is felt by the angry to be justified by their object's badness, is internally generated, and not so much a response to the badness of an object as the cause of it; or, at least, the cause of our idea of it. It is anger seeking an object, and not the other way around.

The point is that anti-Oedipal politics is based on a need to expel unacceptable thoughts and feelings; to project them on to someone else who then can be righteously hated. The problem we see in this case is that such feelings are, ultimately, inseparable from our sense of ourselves as finite and limited human beings. They will always be within us. From this, it follows that the politics driven by anti-Oedipal dynamics will always be a politics of antagonism; it can find no resting place. "I hate, therefore I am" is its *leit motif.*

In the next chapter, we will see how this played out in the destruction of Antioch College. For the present, it is worthwhile to observe that this dynamic obviously poses real limits on the efficacy of a conciliatory response to the politics of political correctness.

CHAPTER FOUR

Antioch against itself: transformation of the meaning of Antioch College

Wednesday, 23 May, 1973

"Congratulations—I hear we won . . ."

W hen the closure of my *alma mater*, Antioch College, was announced on 12 June 2007 there was plenty of *schaedenfreude* to go around (e.g., Will, 2007), but there was considerable sadness as well.

Characteristic was Leon Botstein, the distinguished president of Bard College. Speaking from Jerusalem, where he was music director for the Jerusalem Symphony Orchestra, Botstein called the death "a tragedy that should not have happened" (Jaschik, 2007).

> Antioch College is one of the historic, great, independent colleges in American history. It was the founding college of the American progressive movement. . . . It was a strong, important place. And you know it had distinguished alumni, among them Stephen Jay Gould, and it should never have closed. [*ibid.*]

Yet, for some, it had died a long time ago. Everett K. Wilson (1985), a former member of the Antioch faculty, declared in 1985 that Antioch was already dead.

Of course, he was not speaking literally:

> I use the word, death, metaphorically. The organization persists in attenuated form. But it is such a stranger to its past that it might well be seen as a different organization, displacing its predecessor. It persists only tenuously, reduced in size, resources, and program, without a philosophy of education or a distinctive purpose that would confer identity. [*ibid.*, p. 260]

Still, he did not hold out much hope that it would survive in any form, and it turned out he was right.

On the other hand, whatever this organization in "attenuated form" was, it was vibrant. Faculty and students at the school, in alliance with a revived and committed group of alumni, put up a fight for salvation that gained considerable national attention (Cohen, 2008). That fight was lost, but it is not possible to deny that something was very much alive.

But what was it? Wilson's designation of it as ". . . a stranger to its past . . . a different organization, displacing its predecessor . . . without a philosophy of education or a distinctive purpose that would confer identity" tells us what it was not, but conveys no positive information.

We lose nothing if we simply say that Antioch changed; specifically, the meaning of Antioch changed. In so far as an organization is defined by its meaning, the Antioch that Wilson knew died indeed, but the organization that replaced it had a vitality of its own; along with that, it had a philosophy of education and a distinct purpose. Ultimately unviable it might have been, but as an obituary in the *New York Times* (Cohen, 2008) put it, it certainly did not go gently. (Many of the alumni dispute the College's unviability, claiming that the College could have brought itself to health were it not for the incompetence and hostility of the Antioch University administration. Now is not the time for me to go into this; I will only say two things at this point. First is that the AU administration was competent enough with regard to the rest of the University. Second, that the hostility it bore towards the College was probably not unrelated to the antecedent hatred felt by the College towards the University; a viable College would have found a more constructive way to relate to its environment. In fact, the impulse behind the creation of the University in the first place had its root in the self-destructive psycho-political dynamic I shall describe. Whether it killed Antioch College endogenously or exogenously, through the agency of the University, it killed it none the less.)

Wilson did not recognize it, but that was for a reason. Antioch had redefined itself to be, in fundamental ways, the opposite of what it had been before, and through which Wilson defined what the purpose and philosophy of a college would be.

It had gone from Oedipal to anti-Oedipal. In so doing, it had redefined itself to be against, and destructive towards, what it previously meant.

My purpose in this chapter is to show how this transformation came about and how it affected the viability of Antioch College. For that purpose, I will first revisit the theoretical material, adding what is necessary for this purpose.

Theoretical introduction

As we have seen, for psychoanalytic theory, the process of socialization, of how an individual becomes a member of society, is rooted in the Oedipus complex. In the classic formulation, the Oedipus complex is resolved through introjection. The child brings the father into himself, which means internalizing the impersonal rules of society and the associated understandings of reality, codified in the common meanings embedded in language, which Lacan refers to as the symbolic order.

The core to this commonality is the "paternal function," which is the capacity to see oneself from a standpoint that represents the world's indifference to us and does not give us any special place; it does not belong specifically to any of us, and that therefore is available to all of us. This objective self-consciousness is developed through history, and is constantly under revision through our developing capacity to understand what it means to be a human being.

The objective framework may be said to exist at a number of levels of abstraction. At the highest level, we have reason, logic, and mathematics, which we may think of as the structure of objectivity. These make possible the development of lower levels of abstraction, including the various laws and norms of society, structures of exchange, and understandings of objective reality that can be collectively comprehended, learnt, negotiated, and applied.

Specifically from the standpoint of social relations, the objective framework is what makes it possible to codify and comprehend the network of exchange relationships that form the normative structure of society—a set of widely accepted interlinked hypothetical propositions of the form "If X does this, Y should do that". In such propositions, we can place ourselves either in the X position or the Y position. This has made it possible for people to be mutually predictable and comprehensible to one another and to understand and co-ordinate with each other.

But notice that while something is surely gained in this resolution of the Oedipal complex, something is also lost. What is lost to objectivity is the sense of one's cosmic importance, of being the centre of a loving world that fusion with mother originally meant, which Freud called primary narcissism. "The letter kills," says Lacan (1988). And that is what it kills: the sense that the world is one's own world. The objective framework, in other words, reveals our narcissism to be narcissism.

It stands to the favour of psychoanalytic theory that it can comprehend that what is lost is never really lost. Primary narcissism remains within every one of us and from that perspective, the rage against the father, and, hence, against the social rules, the common understandings, and the whole symbolic order that he represents. This makes possible another formulation of meaning, which we have called anti-Oedipal.

Here, again, a world is structured, but the structure, codified in the language of political correctness, is the mirror image of Oedipal meaning: Expel the father, rather than identify with him, undermine his claims to legitimacy, rather than make sense of them. The phantasy here is that, if we do this, the perfect world of mother's love will be restored.

What I want now to point out is that anti-Oedipal meaning and political correctness can serve as the basis for a politics. Of this politics, which could be identified with what is called "identity politics", two things may be said. First is that there would be the basis of an alliance with the oppressed, which is to say, those whose grievances are, or we believe should be, most deeply felt and profound. This would enhance our hatred of the father and multiply its power.

But it would do so by denying the objective frame and the word's indifference that it represents. Anti-Oedipal politics does not recognize indifference, but only love or hatred. Circumstances that thwart our desires cannot be acknowledged as objective features of our situation, but only as intentional attacks by evil forces.

Second is a structural consideration. Anti-Oedipal politics is essentially nihilistic. Its aim is destruction. Set against the perfect goodness of fusion with mother, nothing can be worthwhile. Indeed, everything that exists stands as a barrier to goodness and is, therefore, bad; it deserves to be destroyed. This includes the rules of exchange that define organization.

But notice that fusion with mother is the only place that it can make sense to get to. Hence, anti-Oedipal meaning can never have the idea of getting anywhere else, and must be an end in itself. The rules and understandings of reality that the father represents, and that have as their Oedipal meaning the objective conditions within which one must fashion one's route to the ego ideal, can have no correlates here. The underlying phantasy is that fusion with mother will be restored if the father is destroyed, but from the standpoint of maintaining a conscious political perspective, the father cannot be destroyed or the basis of meaning disappears. Hence, the basis of meaning for such politics is the continual process of destroying the father.

On the level of politics, this can amount to a very powerful force, but one that is as dangerous to its practitioners as it is to its object. Such a powerful force, directed against organization, can destroy organization, but may do so with a peculiar inadvertance. My hypothesis is that this is what happened to Antioch College.

In so far as it was formulated within Oedipal meaning, Antioch College was destroyed. That is not to say that nothing remained, but it is the reason Wilson did not recognize what Antioch had become. Wilson's model of education was rooted in Oedipal meaning, and on the idea that the father had something to offer.

Yet, the meaning of Antioch had become anti-Oedipal, rooted in the permanent destruction of the father. What remained, in other words, was the very anti-Oedipal politics that destroyed it. It co-opted what was left of Antioch College and, like a hermit crab, took over its structure. Antioch redefined itself as being against itself.

Ultimately, it was doomed. Whatever its vibrancy, in the end it had declared war on reality, and reality always prevails.

Oedipal Antioch

If one wanted to place Antioch on the political spectrum running from right to left, one would always have located it on the left. This is an important point, because it might otherwise be tempting to believe that the left is my object of criticism; it is not. As the statisticians would have it, the dimension that concerns me is orthogonal to the dimension that runs from left to right.

My point is, rather, that the meaning of the left shifted over the history of Antioch. That shift, from social democratic politics, which idealizes a certain social order, to identity politics, which idealizes the self, corresponds to the shift from Oedipal to anti-Oedipal meaning that I would like to elucidate.

The key to Oedipal Antioch is the character of Arthur Morgan, a charismatic figure who was Antioch's president from 1920 to 1935, and who gave the College its unique institutions, such as the work–study programme, in which students spent roughly half their time on full-time co-operative jobs, and the community governance system, in which students participated fully in college governance. He was an engineer, a social progressive, and a full patriarch.

Morgan made this patriarchal function explicit. Writing in the *Atlantic Monthly* (1929) he contrasted Antioch's milieu, which he called "Almus Pater", with the maternal spirit, "Alma Mater", which he had found to dominate other colleges. Both are important, said Morgan, but the father had been neglected. Yet he must be there to provide an external challenge to the students, so that they may learn to deal with a harsh, external reality.

Morgan had no qualms about imposing an objective frame; he had a very definite idea of what education should be about, and he designed Antioch College to realize that idea. That is not to say that the student would be passive matter upon which the College would impose itself. On the contrary, it was inherent in Morgan's vision that the properly formed graduate would be an active shaper of his or her own ideas. What the College intended to impart was the rigour with which such shaping would be done and the experience that would be brought into it, in accordance with the knowledge that would come from the mastery of a curriculum based on the highest accomplishments that had been achieved through the intellectual disciplines. The student was called upon to bring these experiences and understandings into himself and make use of them within his own developing personal orientation towards the world. As Wilson put it, in a case study co-authored with Joan O. Yalman (1985)

> From first to last, the Morgan student was encouraged, indeed required, to think about purpose, about personal philosophy. The person applying for admission wrote about his or her aims in life; and, at exit time, the senior had to write a paper on personal aims and philosophy. In the meantime, in Morgan's day, all Antioch students took a course in philosophy, reinforcing the emphasis on weighing the ends of life and the means of achieving desired ends. Morgan and his faculty stressed a broad exposure to a number of fields of scholarship: required courses in the biological and physical sciences, the social sciences and work in English composition and the humanities. Ability to exploit these fields and, somehow, to integrate them, was tested in a final Comprehensive Examination. [Yalman & Wilson, 1985, p. 575]

A critical part of this was the way political orientation fitted into the Antioch program. Morgan had a certain view of the world, which may be called political; he was a progressive. Antioch, as his vision, may be said to have had that orientation as well, but there was nothing in this that contradicted his patriarchy.

Rather, in keeping with the broadly social democratic politics of the time, Antioch's graduates, it was hoped, would also be progressives and patriarchs. They would transform the objective structure of the world so that it would be more fair and universal, but it would be no less objective. Yalman and Wilson say:

> Morgan's Antioch elite would be inventors, not only in the conventional sense (better mouse traps) but also as social designers, modifying social patterns that were inequitable or otherwise inadequate. He celebrated a socially sensitive imagination together with the disciplined skills of the engineer. He had every conviction that the informed intelligence which designed bridges to specified tolerances, could also design social structures that would define a better world. [*ibid.*, pp. 566–567]

Yet, the expression of that view was implicit, not explicit, as it later became. The idea that the student would adopt the vision of the College was perhaps desired, but it was not directly sought, and certainly such a view was not imposed on the student. The social vision of the student would have to come, or not come, through the individual student's development of his or her own philosophy, in accordance with the demands of rigour and in consideration of the range of experiences, worldly and academic, that were the defining characteristics of an Antioch education. Antioch's function, in accordance with its embrace of the objective function, was to teach students how to think and weigh evidence, not to arrive at a predetermined conclusion.

Implicit in this, as part of Morgan's patrimony, was the encouragement of broad ranges of expression and ideological engagement. The assumption was that the challenge of such intellectual diversity, engaged through rigorous and robust intellectual debate, could only help the individual develop his or her own views. Thus, the patriarchal legacy here was the frame through which a range of views could be encountered, compared, and objectively considered.

This is from a retrospective article in the *Weekly Standard* by Charlotte Allen (2007):

> Although political views at Antioch might have tilted leftward even back then, the students of the 1950s and early-to-mid 1960s prided themselves on their willingness to hear out their more conservative

classmates in lively all-night dorm discussions on politics and philosophy, inspired by professors who encouraged them to test all their assumptions against the evidence. "We were completely respectful of every point of view," recalled Rick Daily, a Denver lawyer who graduated from Antioch in 1968 and is treasurer of the alumni committee that is struggling to save the college from closure. "We even had a Goldwater Republican in our graduating class," Daily said in a telephone interview.

And this is from a retrospective piece by Ralph Keyes (2007), a 1967 graduate who took a job at Antioch in around 1990.

> I remembered Antioch as a lively, demanding institution, full of contentious students and professors. Many, including myself, were ardent left-wingers. Others stood elsewhere on the political spectrum. As we understood it, one's political convictions were beside Antioch's point. Its emphasis was on thinking for one's self and keeping an open mind. "Re-evaluate your basic assumptions in the light of new evidence" was a campus cliché. I felt constantly challenged to justify my points of view. But I didn't assume that reassessing those views would move me left. It might move me to the right, or toward the center, or nowhere at all.

Anti-Oedipal Antioch

The political orientation at Antioch in its last years was still towards the left but the contrast of the way it structured meaning was sharp. The agency of the school was presumed to be expressed through fusion, through love, which was massively represented through the term "community". Difficulties that arose were to be met with, not through objective, rational assessment of causes and consequences, but through imagination and creativity, fostered by the community, here representing the maternal muse. Hence, licence was given to fantasy.

But, like it or not, there is an objective reality and it imposes limits on the life of fantasy. These are first encountered in the form of the father. In anti-Oedipal psychology, he is subsequently the object upon whom they are projected, in one guise or other, and attacked as oppressive.

We can see this at a number of institutional levels, beginning with the organization's ideology. Consider this from the *New York Times* article called "The College that would not go gently" (Cohen, 2008):

> As any student at Antioch College can tell you, our view of reality is socially constructed. What we consider to be truth is often just a reflection of the power structure, a single narrative propounded by a privileged class that must be countered by alternative narratives.

She follows this by saying: "Put simply, there is more than one side to any story".

But this is more distortion than simplification. There may be many sides of the story, but not all of them are allowed to be told. Take away the idea of an overarching objective frame of rules for comparing ideas on their merits, and subjectivity is all that can be left. Under these assumptions, the only way a particular subjectivity can prevail is through power. According to this view, the paternal "power structure", or "privileged class", has monopolized this power in the past, but now it is time for the oppressed to stand up against him with their own power.

In this case, their power is mobilized, not through recourse to logic, but through emotional assault and personal abusiveness.

This abusiveness stood out sharply to most observers. Keyes (2007), for example, writes:

> Even in the midst of routine discussion, students interrupted each other with angry outbursts. Presumably this was part of "calling each other out," a popular campus pastime ("I'm calling you out as a product of privilege," "I'm calling you out for wearing Nikes," etc.).

Such attacks on the established social order, including the global capitalism that locates shoe factories in countries where the wage rate is low, are easily seen as attacks on the patriarchal order, but "calling out" has a deeper form. In some cases, people are called out for referring to, and presumably thinking about, others in ways that they do not use to refer to and think of themselves.

> After getting called out for calling Inuits "Eskimos", an exchange student from Poland conducted a survey of language taboos among

Antiochians. He and a colleague found that anyone thought to have used inappropriate words was liable to be ostracized. One student described being verbally assaulted after she innocently addressed a gay student as a "guy". Many told the surveyors how fearful they were of saying the wrong thing. "If you say something wrong," explained one Antiochian, "other people will have no mercy." [Keyes, 2007]

It is not expected that the person will have drawn a boundary around himself, enabling him to see the ideas that others have of him as being the ideas of others. The result of this would have to be that the ideas that others have of us will be experienced as part of ourselves, and wreak havoc with our sense of identity. It is easy to see why one would feel the need to defend against such ideas. But it is important to see how radical this is. What is under attack is any view of oneself that differs from maternal embrace.

This would include the objective frames represented by college and legal officials.

Students were not the only ones being called out. Soon after he arrived on the campus, in early 2006, President Steven W. Lawry received an e-mail message from an Antiochian that said, "Fuck you, asshole." This was not untypical of campus discourse. When the student newspaper asked readers what they would say to a "narc," [a police officer specializing in narcotics] answers included "Stop snitchin' snitches [an informer] get stitches," and "Die motherfucker Die." [ibid.]

This verbal and interpersonal dynamic may be considered a generalized attack on the paternal function of the College, directly and through its mission. It certainly did damage to the prospects for recruiting and retaining students. Lawry put the matter this way, in his State of the College address of 2006:

[T]here are aspects of today's campus culture that are not conducive to the fullest realization of our educational mission. Radical identity politics and identity-centered discourses, while often drawing attention to mistreatment, unfairness and hypocrisy in our society, also take on a stridency and aggressiveness that too often close down conversation, inhibit learning and send off students who really should be here. [p. 6]

But if the damage done by political correctness had been limited to interpersonal interaction, it would have had limited effect. My point is that something was also taking place at the level of the institution. Consider its effect on teaching, which was the main organization process. This is from Cohen (2008):

> Flare-ups over race, gender, politics and more happen at every campus, but because of Antioch's size and focus, they would end up turning into crises, said Eli Nettles, a mathematics professor and the associate dean of faculty. "You say something and it becomes a public incident."

> Ms. Nettles has been at Antioch eight years, and now is interviewing for jobs. She said she was grateful to have taught at Antioch and was a better teacher for it. But before she got tenure in 2005, she said: "I lived in terror that I was going to say something I didn't even know was offensive. I began to feel uncomfortable with my knowledge of the English language."

> The teaching of statistics suddenly became fraught with political overtones, because research was generally not broken into categories that included "transgendered" or "people of color." A student was offended by Ms. Nettles's reference in class to a statistical study on abortion, because "I didn't discuss how pro-abortion isn't the same as pro-life," she said. It's not that the question isn't valid, Ms. Nettles emphasized, but that a math lecture was not the appropriate place to discuss it.

Statistics is nothing more than the mathematics of applied probability; it is pure objectivity. To disrupt a class on statistics because one finds oneself offended by the choice of an example shows that one has missed the point; one simply does not understand the nature of statistics. To the extent that concern for such challenges determines the way the course is taught, what is being taught is not statistics.

That something else is being taught came through in a message to an Internet list of alumni in which I was participating, though not to great applause, from a former student writing to express her appreciation for Antioch.

> And that is what I love about Antioch the most. Every class was an ethics and morals class. Every class challenged and asked questions

concerning race, gender, class, sustainability, disability, age, geography and on and on. Even math classes. Despite the fact that I can't do ANYTHING without asking these questions (every single goddamn one) every second of every day, to perhaps an unhealthy extent, I am so thankful to have learned that as part of my education at Antioch. And wouldn't trade it for all of the blissful ignorance in the world (and there is a lot . . .)

But the transformation at Antioch involved more than teaching. Notice the way Nettles, whose attachment to Antioch surely says something about the orientation of her politics, "lived in terror" at the thought that somebody would find something she said objectionable. What this indicates is an assault on objectivity that goes beyond the nature of statistics. It says the institution is being structured, not by reliable, objective rules, but by whim. What is under attack is objective order itself.

Yet, the attack against social order was not seen as simply an internal matter. It had its correlate in Antioch's orientation to the external world, as is illustrated by this, from Allen (2007):

> Antioch now might be fairly represented by a September 21 article in the student newspaper, the *Record*, consisting of a gloating account of the invasion by 40 gay and lesbian Antioch students (a full fifth of the current student body) of an evangelical Christian book-signing event at a Barnes & Noble store located in a mall in nearby Beavercreek, Ohio. *Record* reporter Marysia Walcerz described the hours-long "Gay Takeover," whose participants wore rainbow-tinted bandannas, ostentatiously held hands and kissed, and did their best to shock both authors and customers in this socially conservative sector of Ohio, as a "success . . . for direct action executed in style."

Nothing illustrates this better than the choice of their 2000 commencement speaker. This is from Allen again:

> It was, however, the sort of environment in which a convicted murderer and former Black Panther, Mumia Abu-Jamal, could be invited by students to deliver the commencement speech [by tape recording] in 2000. There had been plenty of evidence supporting Abu-Jamal's conviction in 1982 for shooting Philadelphia police officer Daniel Faulkner five times in the face and back at close range—such as the

five spent casings in Abu-Jamal's gun that matched the five bullets lodged in Faulkner's body—and even some leftists have questioned the rush by their fellows to turn Abu-Jamal, currently awaiting the outcome of one of several appeals of his death sentence, into a political prisoner who had been framed by racist cops. When Maureen Faulkner, widow of the slain officer, sent a letter protesting the honor to be conferred on her husband's killer to Robert H. Devine, an Antioch communications professor who had succeeded Crowfoot as the college's president, Devine wrote back, "As educators, it is our responsibility to provide an environment where widely varying points of view can be expressed."

Yet Devine was being disingenuous here. The issue was not whether Abu-Jamal could be heard. He could have been heard in a classroom setting without provoking any furore. The issue was whether he should have been chosen as commencement speaker, and in that way representing the meaning of the institution. Abu-Jamal was a person whose fame was due to the fact that he had been convicted of murdering an agent of the society's legal order. His defence presented a picture in which virtually the entirety of constituted authority in Philadelphia, and the USA generally, was organized as a racist plot to arrest Mumia Abu-Jamal (for a relatively understated expression of this conspiracy theory, see Amnesty International, 2000). The hypostatization of this vast scheme is the only way to discount the evidence against him. One must conclude that choosing him represented an embrace of this view of American society. In choosing him to represent it, Antioch was doing one or both of two things. First, it was repudiating the importance of evidence in formulating judgement. Second, it was defining itself through an expression of hatred towards the social order of the world in which it lived. In both regards, Antioch was establishing itself as being in a state of war with the father.

There are also indications that, not surprisingly, the attack against the father spilled over into the students' relations with the College itself. Lawry (2006) again:

Over many decades, Antioch students have benefited educationally from the opportunity to participate in AdCil and ComCil [these are two community governance bodies, at different levels, each containing members from all elements of the community] and other bodies that give voice to student participation in campus decision-making. . . . Community governance is an important aspect of the Antioch experience, and I support it. However, I have concerns with community governance as it is currently understood and practiced. . . . [T]o my disappointment, there has been a militancy and aggressiveness sometimes directed toward the administration that is really unmerited and not consistent with the educational mission of shared governance structures. [p. 7]

It would be a mistake to believe, though, as Lawry seems to believe, that these anti-Oedipal manifestations were simply features and expressions of the student culture. This is from an article in the *Chronicle of Higher Education*:

> Mr. Lawry, who came from the Ford Foundation, says that by the time he arrived, the college was in the grip of radically leftist students, intolerant of other views. "It chased off students and had a deleterious effect," he says. "The adults were looking the other way." [Carlson, 2007]

In fact, the adults "looking the other way" was also an expression of the organization.

Allen (2007) says something similar, and puts the causality where it belongs:

> The adults who could have and should have intervened to put a lid on the excesses of a culture created by 18- to 22-year-olds with little experience of the outside world in fact let that culture run untrammeled and amok, all in the name of Antioch's vaunted ideal of "community."

Summing up, from the time of Morgan to the time of its demise, we see a transformation of Antioch from Oedipal to anti-Oedipal psychology, a deterioration that ultimately proved fatal.

1973, the declension point

There is no question about when the trajectory of Antioch began its downward turn. That was in 1973, a period during which a strike was held that paralysed the campus for six weeks.

The objective facts of the strike are straightforward. Beginning with a grant from the Rockefeller Foundation, Antioch had been recruiting low-income, primarily black, students, without regard to standard academic selection criteria. The programmes through which this was accomplished changed over time, finally taking the name "New Directions". The number of such students, starting with zero in 1963, rose monotonically to about fifteen per cent of the student body by 1973. Virtually all were on full financial assistance.

In 1973, the Nixon administration was cutting back on its funding for college programmes that were important in providing financial aid, primarily the National Defense Student Loan (NDSL) and Supplemental Educational Opportunity Grant programmes. Most importantly, the NDSL programme, in which colleges themselves administered the loans, which were at three per cent interest, was to be replaced by federally insured loans administered by banks, which would be at seven per cent interest. There was further concern that many students, especially the black students admitted under the New Directions programme, would not be able to obtain these loans, even at the higher rate, due to "their poor credit rating, combined with the racism and class prejudice of most banks" (Abramson, Casey, & Greenfeld, 1973). The College, which was already devoting $1.4 million of its $6.1 million operating budget to financial aid (Yalman & Wilson, p. 326) said that it had, by cutting departmental budgets, set aside an additional $300,000 to take care of these students, and that the level of aid for 1972–1973 would be maintained for 1973–1974, but these were not deemed sufficient. The students demanded a contract stating that their aid would be maintained until graduation. The Administrative Council (AdCil) went along with these demands, but the Trustees did not. They refused to agree to such a contract and the strike was on.

The strike, which garnered considerable publicity, caused extensive property damage. It also saw a large number of students withdraw and cut the number of entering students approximately in half. Going into the strike, Antioch enrolled about 2,500 students. Afterwards, although there were ups and downs, down was the overall trajectory. At the end, there were about 200 students. For a school with very little endowment, and which therefore relied heavily on tuition, this falling off of student attendance was crippling.

Our concern, though, is not historical, but psychoanalytic. We are looking not so much to explain Antioch's changing fortunes as the changing way it made meaning. Our interest in this period is to see whether we can detect the shift from the Oedipal to the anti-Oedipal. Specifically, we want to know what happened to the objective frame.

This takes a very specific form in the study of the strike period. The question is: why could the college not defend itself? Why could it not uphold the objective framework that made it possible to respectfully exchange ideas and learn, subject to the demands of rigorous debate? Why could it not uphold the paternal legacy of Morgan, which defined it?

The answer is that Antioch could not defend its paternal legacy because, through the agency of the strike, Antioch was attacking itself. Antioch had redefined itself as being against itself, and specifically the objective form that hitherto constituted its identity. Antioch was committing suicide.

The strikes of 1973

Trying to understand the way Antioch was making meaning, I looked at the way the campus saw the strike. I turned to contemporary documents, located in the Antiochiana archive on the Antioch campus in Yellow Springs.[1] One thing that became clear in those accounts is that the Antioch community regarded the strike as being one in a series of strikes going back years. None had been so damaging, but the question of why this strike had proved fatal, and the others had not, seemed critical to the understanding of Antioch's self-destruction. It was of particular interest to compare the New Directions strike, which took place in Spring quarter 1973, with a strike of university employees that had taken place in the previous Winter quarter.

The major difference was that, while the Spring strike was about race, the Winter strike concerned labour–management relations. The university, having run annual operating deficits of around $200,000, wanted to subcontract the dining hall operation to an outside company. The employees, massively supported by students and some faculty, struck over the demand that they be able to retain jobs in the dining halls. (Actually, putting the matter this way understates the strength of student involvement in the strike. One of the unions was the Part Time Employees Union, which contained a large number of students. The other was the United Electrical Workers.)

In the end, the administration held to its position. The strike lasted four weeks, but teaching and most administrative processes continued. Occasional acts of violence were prosecuted. Finally, the administration threatened an injunction and a contract was reached. In sum, the paternal structure of meaning prevailed.

For our purposes, the crucial point is that the College stood fast during the Winter strike and collapsed during the Spring strike. The question is, why was this so?

I believe part of the answer is suggested by something from the *Record* coverage. The reporter here is referring to an employee's response to the union's tactic of dumping garbage on the floors of the administration building:

> Non-union supervisors spent much of the afternoon cleaning up from the previous days' garbage melee in main building's lobby and the office of Interim Dean of the College Ewell Reagin.

> Muttering "scab," Manny Durbin, local UE president, strode down the hall knocking over a trash barrel. A few unidentified students dumped much of the remaining trash into the hall.

> One of the supervisors continued methodically loading trash into an incinerator slot in main building, all but ignoring the accusation of "scab" hurled at him. "I've grown up a long time ago," said David Rue, in response to the incident. Helping strew garbage is "the first work Manny's done for three weeks," he added in disgust.

> According to College Negotiator John Sullivan, Rue does not qualify as a scab because traditionally, in time of emergency, supervisors have done work normally done by union workers. Loose trash is considered a health danger, and therefore an "emergency." [Howard, 1973, p. 1]

Why was it important whether David Rue was properly called "scab", and why was it important for John Sullivan to define the term for those around him and for the *Record*? I suggest it was because in our society there are highly developed rules for such strikes, and the strike would play out in accordance with them. Individuals who were partisans of the strike were partisans of the strike *defined in that way*. These rules were themselves part of the paternal order, and they gave the administration a defined role within which to operate, a ground on which they could stand, which the supporters of the strike accepted, whether they liked it or not, because it was within the meaning of being on strike.

By contrast, the Spring strike was about race and had no rules; it was, therefore, bound to be determined by the underlying emotions. Understanding the Spring strike, then, means understanding those emotional forces. That will be our task in what follows.

In getting a handle on the motivation for the strike, it should first be observed that there were real issues here, on both sides. The students, who had been recruited with the full knowledge that they were poor and would have to be fully subsidized, felt that the College had made a commitment to them that it was not prepared to honour. The College, which had counted on outside founding that was being cut back, knew itself to be in desperate financial condition and knew that making such a guarantee would probably result in bankruptcy. As always, though, the immediate issue of the strike cannot be understood without a sense of where it came from, both historically and emotionally. From a psychoanalytic point of view, these cannot help but be intertwined. Some background is therefore necessary.

History of the black student movements at Antioch

From its beginning, Antioch, following directly from its vision of itself, had a tradition of seeking out black students. The project, in co-operation with the Rockefeller Foundation, called the Antioch Program on Interracial Education (APIE), however, differed in the type of students who were recruited.

> APIE students differed from the blacks who had preceded them. Not all had been well to do, but there was some college or university experience in their backgrounds and, above all, one criterion in their selection had been demonstrated achievement in earlier schooling. Names often mentioned as representing the triumphs of

this earlier group of black Antioch students are the psychiatrist, Lonnie McDonald, the federal judge, Leon Higginbotham, the New York civic leader and official Eleanor Holmes Norton [now Congressional Representative from the District of Columbia], and a person influential in the civil rights movement, Corrie Scott, who became Mrs Martin Luther King. [Yalman & Wilson, p. 300]

That changed with the APIE.

Nearly three-fourths of them were male. They came from fairly large families, half of which were broken by death, divorce, or separation, and "several students had separated themselves completely from their families" (Graham, 1967, p. 10). A third of the fathers were unemployed or deceased (or their whereabouts unknown), another third were labourers, the rest service workers and operatives. Among the mothers, a third were housewives, a tenth were deceased, a fifth were labourers, and the rest were fairly evenly spread among service, domestic, and clerical work. Family earnings for a fourth of them were under $3,000, a third had earnings between $3 and $5 thousand dollars. (None earned more than $7,000.) No parent contributed more than $400 to the student's support and thirty contributed less than $100.

Not only were the APIE students from poor families; their parents and siblings were likely to have had little formal schooling. "Most of the fathers and mothers", Graham reports (1967, p. 10) "had no more than a high school education, and many had less". [*ibid.*]

From the beginning, there appears to have been a difference in the way the Rockefeller Foundation and Antioch conceived of the programme.

For the Rockefeller Foundation people, the aim was to reach Negroes with apparent talent and special promise. In the discussion of the Foundation Board of Trustees on 1 April 1964, the Minutes speak of "the movement of education for those Negroes and other minority group members who are more likely to be—or with encouragement can rapidly become—outstanding leaders among their own groups and in the nation. For this purpose special efforts are required to provide enlarged opportunities and increased encouragement for Negro and other students of high potential to benefit from the best that our system of higher education has to offer". [*ibid.*, p. 296]

Clearly, the Rockefeller people hoped that the most able and promising black students might be identified and thereupon furnished with the best possible undergraduate education (*ibid.*).

In other words, the Oedipal programme was fully in play. For the Antioch administration, however, things were a bit different. This is from a book of transcribed interviews with James P. Dixon, who was president at the time:

> . . . one school of thought . . . argued for a pretty careful selection of students. . . . I don't think Dudley [Dawson, Dean of Students] said we should select for success [*sic*] . . . But I think he thought we should be careful about our social class boundaries. But there were other people in the college . . . who felt that if one were to address the issue, and open the institution up to its possibilities—why would one be so careful as to select merely those who were likely to succeed? [Dixon, 1991, p. 130]

Of course, the intention was not to bring in students entirely without selection. These were the qualities considered important:

> courage, realism, imagination, skill in communication, past success in any area, stubborness and tenacity, toughness (a sense of self and worth), intellectual and emotional accessibility (openness) freedom of mind, independence of judgment, sense of humor, ability to work hard, a complicated mind. [Yalman & Wilson, p. 298, citing Graham, 1967]

But these attributes had nothing specific to do with intellectual activity and their relationship to academic success was only fanciful. They were also difficult to assess, especially by those who, in reality, had little relationship with prospective candidates.

Summing up, Yalman and Wilson say,

> Thus these students were selected first because of race (or minority status); second because of need; third because of certain inferred qualities such as imagination or realism; but not at all for such predictors of success or promise as might reside in academic achievement or other signs of intellectual accomplishment. They were referred to as high risk students. [*ibid.*, p. 299]

Bringing students into an otherwise highly selective and rigorous institution, and one which was as different from these students' experience and culture as could be imagined, was a prescription for alienation and failure. This is built into the very term "high risk", which is an expression of probability, and means high probability of failure. These students were known to do badly on the criteria that had been associated with relative success. In choosing to select students because they were high risk, the College was choosing those students who were expected to fail. That is, of course, what happened.

Yalman and Wilson quote from a 1968 study by Professor Lois Sparks of "Separatism at Antioch: a study of the Antioch interracial education program".

> Sparks compares 25 middle and upper-middle class white students randomly drawn from the entering class in the fall of 1965 with all APIE students entering in the summer and fall of 1966 (N=24).

> Reading the responses of APIE students to her questionnaire, Sparks says . . . that

>> one gets the feeling that most of them arrive at Antioch with only the dimmest comprehension of what a college is all about. Since they never really expected to go to college, they have not, unlike the regular students, acted out the college experience in their imaginations or informed themselves about alternatives. When they enter, therefore, Antioch is little more than a place (and a fairly exotic one) which may or may not serve their physical and social needs. But at that early stage, they are unequipped even to define the educational program, much less assess their own attitudes toward it. [*ibid.*, pp. 301–302]

At the same time:

> Sparks notes that APIE blacks bring with them an identity, a commitment to a cause, "... an already strong sense of social and cultural distance which [they] feel almost from their first hour on the Antioch campus" (Sparks, 1968: 20). The distance is not only a matter of racial experience and stereotypes: it is confounded with— compounded by—class ... Negro students who enter Antioch through regular channels resemble, in these respects, white students who enter with them. The point is that *the APIE students embody disprivilege compounded*, a new phenomenon at Antioch, and one with which the total program as currently constituted may be

only minimally prepared to cope" (Sparks, 1968: 2, italics added). [Yalman and Wilson, p. 301]

In summing up a set of observations, Sparks concludes (1968, p. 17) that:

We have in the APIE group, then, more people who exhibit low self esteem; defensive control of impulse, emotion, and fantasy; rigid conceptions of self; and a cautious, mistrustful view of others. Small wonder that interpersonal empathy and unselfconscious exchange comes hard, when the respective zeitgeists of so many students are so manifestly at odds. [Yalman and Wilson, p. 302]

Yalman and Wilson continue:

One difficulty in the adjustment of organization to client, and vice versa, was the sheer rapidity of the increase in number of students who differed so dramatically from those hitherto admitted . . . At the beginning, each of a small number of black students was treated pretty much as an individual case. But with a substantial increase in numbers this was less possible; and there were enough blacks to unite in the face of their common problems—problems largely unanticipated by a white, middle class faculty and administration (whose experience had been with high achieving middle class black students); or problems which, when and if anticipated, were ineptly dealt with.

We do not suggest that the problems were simple For these students the heritage of racism and poverty meant that they necessarily imported to Antioch special handicaps for learning—a lack of will, suspicion, a preemptive concern with race which was encouraged by national events as well as conditions within the College. Although most had both the ability and the desire to learn, they lacked the will, the determination, the self-discipline to do so. They also brought with them, Graham says, "a kind of wariness of authority and suspiciousness of the white middle class that [precludes] that modicum of trust needed in a learning situation." And, she adds, they have "a preoccupation with [identity] which saps the energy, takes time, and forecloses concentration on matters that lie outside their concern with being poor and/or black. These factors seem to be more acute for the males than for the females" (Graham, 1967: 23). And added to all this is the sense that the

Antioch program is irrelevant. "Antioch is, after all, an academic community and . . . academics, narrowly conceived as the trans-mission of culture . . . will seem least useful for the needs of these young people whose experiences thus far have prepared them for living a different kind of life" (Graham, 1967: 20).

One is not surprised, then, when Graham says (1967: 14) that for APIE students "the transition [to Antioch] was sufficiently unset-tling [to be described as culture shock] . . . The students were unprepared for [the differences] they found in language, customs, values, artifacts" . . . [ibid., pp. 304–305]

Continuing with Yalman and Wilson:

Under these conditions it was easy for initial respect and anxiety to turn into hostility and contempt. The APIE students come with the knowledge that Antioch students are the cream of the crop—smart, wise, and rich. Their first reaction is awe, to which reaction they cling for a while despite the casual dress and because of the verbal virtuosity of the students. After a while this turns to hostility, the hostility the outs have for the ins, and later to contempt as they begin to learn about the usual Antioch student hangups, problems that seem to be unreal artifices, made up for effect (Graham, 1967: 17).

Graham has the impression that this hostility escalated at the end of the quarter as pressures and tensions mounted. At such times, especially, the APIE "students tend to view other students as phony, the Program staff as bumblers, and the College as impossi-ble." [ibid., pp. 305–306]

The result could surprise no one:

Among black students, dissatisfaction with the academic program grew—its irrelevance, its fix on Angloamerican culture and white, middle class America. It was not expressed in these terms: it was a product of anxiety and frustration coupled with an ignorance of the connection between these means and desired ends. [ibid., p. 311]

Faced with all these problems, and in the absence of any effective response from the organization, students took the solution into their own hands. Finding the host College unacceptable, they raided its resources to create their own. [ibid., p. 310]

This took a number of forms, beginning with demands for separate living facilities, then proceeding to a separate curriculum, increased funding, control over that increased funding, a larger black cohort, greater control over organizational decision making, and so on.

Yalman and Wilson put it this way:

> In his book, *Enemies of Promise*, Cyril Connolly tells about a Georgian boyhood, his experiences, commencing at age 11 or 12 at St. Wulfric's, a private school preparing its students for such public schools as Harrow and Eton . . . through a traditional pattern of age-ranked privilege, faculty and administrators coopted older students to sustain an intricate set of beliefs, values, behavior and authority. Hazings, canings, fear and favors were expected to build character while the classics, literature, mathematics and history were to produce respect for tradition and skills of literacy.

> In an inversion of this process, blacks at Antioch coopted the College. Young blacks took over the elders, the weak instilled fear in the strong. They made stipulations affecting admissions, housing, their curriculum and means of assessing progress. Indeed they took over the meaning of the degree. [*ibid.*, pp. 310–311]

Yet, focusing on the motivations of the black students explains both too little and too much. It brings us to a point at which we can have what Weber called "sympathetic understanding". The truth is that they had been placed in a situation that was absolutely intolerable, and their reaction to this circumstance made perfectly good sense. Stopping at this point might easily give us a feeling that we have understood the strike and the destruction of the College.

But two obvious questions remain. First, the black students never represented more than a minority on campus: about fifteen per cent at the time of the strike, but for most of the period, far fewer than that. More interestingly, in the strike itself, they represented only a minority. The motivations of the majority of the strikers have not been explained; if it was the black students who were pursuing their advantage through the strike, how could the participation of the whites, who were not only students but faculty, be understood? They were the majority, yet they seem peripheral. Second, we have the fact that the response of the black students was one that anybody could have predicted. When the College undertook to bring so many unprepared students, especially coming from a cultural milieu so hostile to the white middle-class element that Antioch, like it or not, would be taken to represent, they were either being remarkably stupid or they were asking for trouble. Yet, they were not stupid people at all, which leads us towards the second explanation. But what was the meaning of the trouble for which they were asking? Here, we understand too little.

These are both questions for which psychoanalytic theory is well suited to provide answers. The answers I will propose are that, in the first place, the motivations of the white strikers were not peripheral. In reality, it was a white middle-class strike all along. And the reason the College was asking for trouble is precisely because trouble was what they wanted. The strike was their own exercise. That was why they could not uphold the objective frame; they had organized themselves against it. To be sure, the black students were involved in the strike, but they were involved as instrument, rather than as cause. Through them, Antioch was killing itself. I will return to this after a while. First, it will be necessary to explore the Spring strike.

Psychodynamics of the Spring strike

Getting a handle on the Spring strike, and understanding how it was different from the Winter strike, is made both more difficult and easier by the fact that the personnel at the *Record*, upon whom we rely for contemporary views, were an entirely different crew than they were during Winter. This was an immediate result of the fact that a division change had taken place between studying and working off campus at co-operative jobs. More important was that, for reasons I do not know, they defined themselves differently. They called themselves a "collective" and took on an explicitly ideological orientation. They adopted a style, common to the communications organs of radical political groups, such as the *Daily Worker*, in which there is an obliteration of the boundary between fact and interpretation, and in which the interpretation always assumes the legitimacy and wisdom of the political group. Much of the space in the paper was given over to the coverage of labour strikes and other political struggles elsewhere.

The change in voice by the *Record* poses problems for comparing the strikes of 1973, in so far as the *Record's* reporting is concerned. It does, however, give us direct access to the way the strike was seen by those sympathetic to it, and to the construction of meaning within that perspective. Of particular interest in this will be the way the motivation behind the strike was understood.

The strike supporters' position

As I have said, the bulk of the strikers were not the New Directions students themselves, but their white middle-class supporters, both among students and faculty. Yalman and Wilson discuss the transformation that had been taking place among these groups, largely in terms of an increase in the number of radicals. Considerations of space preclude dealing with that here, and, in any case, our interest is not so much in who these radicals were, but in what radicalism meant.

What is of interest from our point of view is the way the strike's supporters interpreted the strike, which we may gather from the position taken by the *Record*. What is most apparent is the way the issue was moralized, and, indeed, in absolute terms. The College and the Nixon administration both represented the same bad force. We know who the force is from the general theory of political correctness. It is the father, who has stolen mother's love and keeps on doing so. He has deprived the oppressed black students in the past, and now he is doing it again. They now demand that what has been stolen should be restored; mother is standing up in their defence. This moral issue is the only issue; everything else is just a paternal smokescreen.

Turning to the specifics of the case, this is how the *Record* understood the decision to go on strike:

> By the beginning of this quarter the patience of the New Directions and financial aid students had begun to wear thin. Facing a national government that valued corporate profits more than the human rights of poor and working people, was difficult at best, but when added to a college administration that was insensitive and indifferent to their needs the situation became impossible. [Abramson, Casey, and Greenfeld, 1973, p. 1]

The constraints faced by the College were not an issue, and the claim that there were constraints was a lie. The only issue was who should have power. The cause of the strike was the administration's badness and its hypocrisy. Their legitimacy was not recognized; they were only acting in the interest of the white and rich. The poor and black, because they were poor and black, should rule. This is from an editorial of May 11:

> The whole question of economic possibilities—whether money "exists"—is essentially misleading. It is decisions about where money is spent, decisions which are political in nature, which are at the base of the strike. The New Directions program was popular to undertake when there was a lot of foundation and Federal money around, but now that those funds are drying up, so is the College's commitment to the program.
>
> What is at issue is the question of power—can the administration break this strike, as they tried to break the UE–PTEU strike last quarter, and assert total authority over the College in the future? "Creative conflict" used to be Dixon's theory, but now that the crunch has come, it's time to clear out the "trouble-making elements," those people who have taken the lead in opposing the College's retreat from a progressive posture and its replacement by world-wide expansion, even if it means a return to a white upper-middle class campus.
>
> "Financial considerations" obviously do not represent the real stumbling-block to a strike settlement. Rather, it is Antioch's unwillingness to commit its own funds to guarantee continued educations for New Directions students, and the administration's refusal to negotiate a settlement which would infringe on their power to govern at their whim.

A second current, no less interesting from a psychoanalytic point of view, is that the administration has sinned by putting the New Directions students through a hassle. In an unsigned article called Background to Struggle, they say:

> It has been a little over a year since the Administration was last forced to deal with the issue. The entire community from faculty and trustees to students and administrators has agreed with the abstract idea of "cultural pluralism." But every quarter, the New Directions program and poor students have been forced to struggle

for the same rights over and over again, rights which should be guaranteed for *all* students, regardless of nationality or economic background—enough money to live on, travel to co-op jobs, and buy books to study with, as well as remedial programs and the security of their status as students.

A year ago, the administration stated that New Directions was its first priority. Yet New Directions students are still lacking any solid assurances that their presence at Antioch is secure. The current strike is meant to renew its commitment to New Directions and financial aid students. It is designed so that these problems can be cleared out of the way to allow *all* students a chance to return to the process of getting an education. [20 April, p. 4, emphasis in original]

The idea that education should be hassle free, and, indeed, anxiety free, is offered again in an op-ed piece called "Perspective on the strike" by strike-supporting assistant professor of sociology Marge Nelson, who contrasts the experience of New Directions students with white middle class ones, and says that the heart of the matter is

the right to high quality education without constant fear and hassle. I question whether we can talk about quality education at all unless the student has a sense of economic security and adequate leisure for reflection. The many problems of having to approach a bank that is hostile to the poor, to minorities, and to women, of being forced to take on additional interest, of the constant struggle for security on this campus all seem to relate to the basic right of education. . . .

While it is true that we did come up with funds trimmed out of other programs, the existence of these funds alone was not sufficient. At this point I blame the administration for not sitting down with these students and working over the other equally important problems. Thus anxieties increased—adding to a long history of anxiety on campus. Finally the students felt that they had been forced to act.

. . . The poor and the minorities demand that that the right to attend classes is theirs as well. And that means that this right is not to be interfered with by unnecessary trips to the Bursar's office, changing policies or even constant meetings to deal with the problems. [27 April, p. 3]

(Introducing Marge Nelson's comment, the *Record* offers this:

> This week we attempted to solicit faculty opinion on the strike. Marge Nelson responded affirmatively to our request, but we found it impossible, despite a vigorous search, to find a faculty member with a differing opinion on the strike who was willing to print his [her] viewpoint this week. Hopefully we will be able to print such a comment next week.)

But freedom from anxiety resides in the womb, or otherwise in the phantasy of the close connection with an omnipotent and loving mother with whom we are fused. Consider here Chasseguet-Smirgel's (1986) definition of the ego ideal:

> In my view, this fantasy corresponds to the wish to rediscover a smooth universe without obstacles, roughness or difference, identified with a mother's insides to which one can have free access, the representation, at the thinking level, of a form of unfettered mental functioning with the free circulation of psychic energy. [p. 30]

Saying that this condition is one to which we are entitled essentially says that the demands of reality, and of the separation that, in reality, marks our existence, represent an intolerable imposition. It is not occasioned by any kind of necessity, but is just the result of a malevolent will. In saying this, we cast the father, who represents this reality, in the role of the bad guy.

Smiting this bad guy, showing he is a hypocrite who only pretends to act for the common good, destroying his power to determine events but instead leaving the necessities to the fusion of people "negotiating" with each other, whereupon everybody, and not just the white middle-class that the father represents, can live life free from anxiety, is what the strike is intended to bring about. Mother can and should prevail.

This, then, is what the strike is really about. It is a bid for hegemony on the part of the maternal force, seeking to undermine and delegitimize the paternal. A number of other features of the strike support this analysis, which I will briefly discuss.

First is that the strike itself had become a sacred object. Attempts on the part of the administration to gain the upper hand were viewed not as moves that are part of the game, but almost as acts of sacrilege. For example, consider a response to an administration threat in a 16 May memo from Dean Reagin, which established cut-off dates for laying off striking workers and gaining access to buildings to retrieve files. Bringing the heat of its prose to a maximum, the *Record* issued an editorial entitled "A reprehensible ploy," which said, among other things:

This latest administration ploy is the most reprehensible act we have seen in all the years we have been at Antioch. The administration has struck out at those in the college community least able to bear the financial load that Reagin has delivered to them. The workers soon will be without a means of supporting their families because the administration has decided they must carry the brunt of maintaining a strike-breaking college . . . The strategy of the administration now is to set up an alternative, strike-breaking campus away from campus and in the process try to split the students, faculty and workers in separate, hostile camps. . . . It was a serious mistake for the administration to make it obvious that negotiations broke down because of politics. The admission that finances were not the question and the continuing emphasis on the strike and how to break it have only strengthened our resolve to continue this strike. We are no longer fighting for just our right to education. We are fighting against every administrative use of arbitrary power against poor and working class students, against women, against the workers, against "troublemaking" faculty. We are fighting for the rights of the union, for women's studies, for contracts for faculty who serve our needs, for the quality of our education. All of these will be in constant jeopardy if the administration can crush this strike. WE HAVE LONG BEEN ENGAGED IN THIS STRUGGLE AND WE KNOW THE STAKES ARE HIGH—WE WILL WIN.

As I have said, the maternal, by itself, cannot establish meaning, in the sense of language that can provide a sense of direction. It can only do so by appropriating such language from elsewhere, which is to say from the father. In this case, it does so by negation. Yet, for that reason, conflict with the father is when it comes most alive. It realized itself fully in this strike, turning it into a world-historic struggle that establishes its own cosmic importance.

One can see in this that there is going to be a real problem for the administration. The forces supporting the strike, though not necessarily the New Directions students who initiated it, have come to their highest fulfilment in the strike. Their interest is not in settling the strike, but in maintaining it.

One can see this again at the end of the strike, when a small number of students gained an injunction to end the occupation, which brought outside police forces to bring down the barricades. The *Record* editorialized, on 1 June:

> Those who walked the mass picket lines yesterday realize that the only effect of this injunction will be a very brief calm. It's clear that reopening the buildings does not at all mean the end of the strike— the struggle will continue until it is won.

Of course, the strike did end, as anyone could see it would, but one can easily understand the strike supporters' difficulty in acknowledging that would happen. They had never been so much alive.

A related point is that the College, as an organization, does not really exist for the strike supporters; it only exists as an immoral force, identical with whatever other agencies represent and embody that force. We have seen this already in the way the *Record* has intermingled the struggle at Antioch with similar struggles around the country and the world. What I point to now is the fact that an organization, as a system of exchange, is at the same time a pattern of constraints that is part of Oedipal meaning. Refuse that meaning and you lose the concept of the organization as well. Maintaining that pattern of exchange simply does not register as a purpose within their anti-Oedipal meaning. The idea that, though they depended on it utterly, they might kill it, as they did, did not enter into their calculations.

The administration position

But if the position of the strike supporters is, psychodynamically, rather straightforward, the position of the administration is not. The strikers and their supporters, after all, were just striking. If they failed to comprehend the administration position, that is not all that surprising. They were, after all, on strike. Maintaining the administration's position was not their job. The question that arises in this case is why the administration failed to maintain its position. That was their job; their failure to do so is what is most interesting about this situation.

When I say that the administration failed to maintain its position, I am not simply saying that they failed to use their legal authority to keep the College functioning. They could have immediately gained the injunction that the students finally gained after six weeks. The activities of the strikers, in shutting down the buildings and preventing faculty and staff from functioning, were illegal, not to mention the fires and other destruction that took place. But, in fact, through its history of strikes, Antioch had never called in the police. They would certainly have thought of it as their failure if they had done so.

They would have been right, but the failure would not have been in calling in the police. It would have been in creating the necessity to do so. Antioch's failure was not that it physically could not defend itself, but that it could not morally do so. Antioch could not make its case.

It is useful to again compare the administration's responses in the Spring and Winter strikes. In the Winter strike, Antioch could maintain its position. There was no doubt about where they stood. They acted with confidence and no one doubted that they would do what they said they would do. As we know, this did not find full favour. The *Record*, for example, accused them of dropping their liberal veneer, but they understood the administration's position and accepted its legitimacy. In that event, calling in the police was unnecessary; the administration prevailed through its moral force.

In the Spring strike, by contrast, the administration had no confidence in what it was doing. It could not assert its position and make a case for itself. This was noticed by many observers at the time and in retrospect.

In a general way, a contemporary article in the *New York Times* (Kneeland, 1973) put the matter quite nicely when it said, "In an old satiric definition, a liberal is a person who cannot take his own side in an argument. That, in a way, is Antioch's dilemma".

Leonard Botstein, who was not there, but was familiar with the dynamics of the issue, said,

> Well I think one of the things that Antioch failed in the late sixties was to be able to engage in a critical dialogue with its own students . . . the issue was that somehow the faculty and the administration of Antioch was not able to mount a discussion or defense. [Jaschik, 2007]

One could easily personalize this, laying it at the feet of President Dixon. For example, Allen (2007), seeing it as part of his style, said,

> The guiding spirit behind all the conflict—if "guiding" could be said to be the appropriate adjective—was Antioch's 15th president, James Payson Dixon, a 1939 graduate of Antioch whose 16-year reign, from 1959 to 1975, spanned both the college's apex in prestige and its nadir . . . Dixon had been a focused and energetic administrator during his early years, but his philosophy during the late 1960s seemed to be "Whatever."

We will return to Dixon, but I think it is more interesting and revealing to see it as a systemic failure, of which Dixon's fecklessness was representative. Thus, even those among the students and faculty who wanted to end the strike could not stand against the strikers and in favour of the administration, such as it was. This is from a retrospective in the *Yellow Springs News*:

> At one point a group of 100 faculty and students reopened McGregor Hall, the gym, the library and the science building. Members of the group issued an undated memo saying that they were "concerned with the educational and financial survival of the institution" and that *they were acting neither in favor of the administration nor against the strikers.* [La Croix, 2003, my emphasis]

Similarly, on 19 May, a large and representative meeting of all elements of the community formed an Emergency Committee on the Future of Antioch College, which was intended to prepare information for a forthcoming meeting of the Board of Trustees. They took the step of declaring neutrality on the strike.

Indeed, ambivalence seemed to be a matter of administration policy. At a meeting of faculty on 1 May, Interim Dean Reagin said, according to an unsigned article in the *Record* of 4 May, that

> the two main guidelines he had to follow in bringing the strike to resolution were the balancing of the Yellow Springs campus budget and a continuing commitment to cultural pluralism.

> When asked which of these principles would take precedent if they came into conflict during the resolution, Reagin declined comment.

Bear in mind that "cultural pluralism" is not a phrase occurring in a vacuum. It means, essentially, the New Directions programme, as defined by the Steering Committee to Increase Antioch Pluralism (SCIAP) in 1970, and then redefined in action. Within the context of that meaning, Yalman and Wilson said,

> [T]he pluralism advocated by SCIAP turned out, in its political manifestations, to be the injured vs the privileged, blacks vs. whites, new program (NDP) vs. old. It became, that is to say, a simple opposition of good against evil. [p. 330]

And who, in this instance, was therefore set off as the evil, if not the College itself?

In this context, a focus on Dixon's leadership is especially revealing. This is from the article in the *Times*:

> As the strike has dragged on . . . there are those who say they fear for the survival of its liberal tradition as much as they do for the continuance of the school itself.

> One of these is Dr. Dixon, the heavy-set baldish president. He contends that the aid package is no longer the issue, that the two-year offer the college made is as far as it can go, because it does not have cash to make "guarantees" beyond that time.

> What is at issue now, he said, is the strike itself . . .

> "Lurking in the background is the question of survival," he said, sprawling comfortably in a chair in a short-sleeved knit shirt, "but in the foreground is what kind of survival, since Antioch really doesn't make a fetish of survival or it would never have been behaving the way it's been behaving for the last decade. I don't think the campus would want to survive at any cost.

> "I'm beginning to believe that the level of coercion is destructive of the pluralistic dissent that the campus has been willing to tolerate," Dixon said.

> But since Antioch has always shunned the use of force, Dixon conceded that the situation remains "kind of a standoff." [Knee land, 1973]

"Standoff", was it? This was not a stable situation in which two opposing forces were balanced. The longer the strike went on, the more the reputation and prospects of the College suffered. Beyond some point, the damage would be irreversible.

What was at issue was the existence of the College itself, as Dixon acknowledged. Arrayed against the College were forces that were directed towards its destruction, and whose meaning was best served through the continuation of the strike, not its settlement; and Dixon could not bring himself to choose between them.

The issue, then, was a choice between Oedipal and anti-Oedipal meaning. This is a point whose importance cannot be overemphasized. Oedipal and anti-Oedipal meaning are not two different forces that can be balanced; they are two fundamentally different orientations towards the world. These were two masters that could not both be served. One could not say that the school was making certain accommodations in order to keep students within Oedipal Antioch. Reaching a new objective structure was not the point. The point of the strike was the strike itself; it *was* anti-Oedipal Antioch. By refusing to end the strike, Dixon was permitting it to continue in this manifestation, and helping to assure that its dynamics would be long lasting.

By giving the strikers leave to determine the course of events within the College, the College was essentially defining itself against itself; it was committing suicide.

Antioch against itself

Putting the matter that way, we can see that Antioch was not committing suicide only through the strike. Rather, the strike was the culmination of the whole ten-year period that led up to it. The whole period was a prolonged programme of suicide, of killing the father.

One particular phase stands out here. This was the period in 1969 and 1970 during which the black students, who had gained the College's acquiescence in the establishment of separate living facilities, agreed to give that up in exchange for a shift of resources, including greatly accelerated minority recruitment. They first gained the acquiescence of the students, faculty, and administration, and then took the matter to the Board of Trustees.

The Board was not unanimous. Interestingly, it was a number of minority trustees who took a more conservative view:

On the whole there was greater uncertainty about opening admissions to minority students on the Yellow Springs campus than there was about programs in the system. Some minority board members seemed to favor a less radical approach than the one on which the institution was embarked. They were more inclined to press on the importance of scholarship as opposed to the importance of becoming a person in a social and political sense; less tolerant of confusion and violence; more caring about the reputation of the institution; more sensitive to the issues of first and second class education; more sensitive to the possibility that minority students were being exploited.[2] [Dixon, 1991, p. 147]

But, in the end, the Board agreed with the new policy.

A particularly important element of this was the advent of the New Directions programme itself. Students would be high risk, and "agents of fundamental social change". After a three-day strike, the "Trustees, Adcil, the faculty, and students all agreed that pluralism combined with a fundamentally new direction for the college (not just the New Directions program itself) was to receive priority in planning, and therefore in funding." (*Record*, 12 December 1970; cited in unsigned article "Background to struggle", *Record* 20 April).

This is from the minutes of the Trustees meeting:

... the Board of Trustees heard from AASI [Africa–American Studies Institute] and APIE [Antioch Program on Interracial Education] leaders and endorsed the overall direction of a series of proposals that would lead to bringing in more high risk students, both black and white. What was being sought was a "critical mass" of differently prepared students so that Antioch would have to move in new educational directions to meet their needs. [cited in Yalman & Wilson, p. 436]

Yalman and Wilson comment,

What is remarkable in this statement is that new departures in education were to be brought about, not through a discussion by faculty, or Educational Policy Committee; not through discussion of student needs, learning goals and more effective ways of achieving them: a new scheme of education was to be produced through a demographic ploy. A change in the size and character of the student body would necessitate a "move in new educational directions to meet their needs." It is not clear who would define those needs; but the implication is that those doing the defining would not be the existing faculty who had been defining such needs for some time. One must suppose that the definition of need would be offered by students themselves; and that the outcome would be much as it was under the regime of the AASI. Perhaps this difference was foreseen: instead of a segregated curriculum, segregated faculty, a dual system of evaluation, with a sufficiently changed student body, there would be but one system, that appealing to the needs and capacities of the underdog. [*ibid.* pp. 436–437]

Anti-Oedipal Antioch

As the College's identity went through this transformation, necessarily everything within it changed. From Oedipal meaning, in which the purpose was to offer the objective framework for internalization into the self, Antioch's meaning became anti-Oedipal, in which the purpose was to attack the objective framework. For example, as Yalman and Wilson put it with regard to curriculum:

> [T]he content of this liberal arts education shifted to race, class and politics. Race and class, as the hinges of inequity, dominated all else and became, additionally, the bases for claims on resources and the axes of antagonism. For the many students centrally involved, these concerns simply superseded a range of interests in the humanities—philosophy, literature, the arts; and the biophysical sciences; and, indeed, the social sciences. [*ibid.*, p. 336]

And, generally:

> There was a . . . related change in the culture of this academic community. The change in valued ends (now liberation of the deprived) and in means of achieving ends (aggression) was accompanied by a depreciation of old ends and means. The stress on academic achievement came to be irrelevant, indeed a handicap along the way to political successes. To the extent that this view prevailed, most of the faculty and some interdeterminate part of the student body were without purpose or a valued role.

They add:

> Of course the depreciation of the establishment at home (faculty and administrators) had its counterpart in depreciation of the estab-

lishment abroad—Nixon and his administration in Washington, together with the venture in Vietnam. [*ibid.*, p. 335]

And that goes along nicely with our point. The patrimony of the College was seen as being of a piece with the objective framework of the nation, and all seen as identical with oppression. They were all the father, doing what the father does. Attacking him was what Antioch had undertaken to be.

What remained of Antioch was Antioch in name only: a simulacrum, rather than a fact. Or, one might say it was Antioch, but not Antioch College: Antioch Cult, perhaps.

As for the anti-Oedipal forces that destroyed it, they were simply turned into attacks upon politically incorrect individuals, or towards the world, politically incorrect as, of necessity, it is.

But why?

But in all of this, there is an unanswered question: where was the power of the patriarchal forces, and why were they not able to defend themselves? The point I have been trying to make is that the history of Antioch, beginning in the 1960s, represented an attack against these forces, including their representation in the College itself. Hence, it witnessed a transformation of the meaning of the institution, ultimately leading to its demise. Why was it not able to defend itself?

In a sense, this is the question with which we started out, and one which, on the surface at least, we are no closer to resolving. We have seen the anti-Oedipal dynamic overcome the Oedipal dynamic, and we have seen that the institution itself used that anti-Oedipal dynamic to destroy the paternal framework that, hitherto, had been its identity. In that sense, it committed suicide. But who commits suicide, and why? It seems, again, that this question is unanswered.

But I think we can get closer to the answer by considering a dimension we have not considered. That dimension is sex.

Sex and the politics of sex

Yalman and Wilson point to a singular fact that has been mentioned but that, so far, has gone unremarked, which is that the preponderance of the APIE students were male.

This is a peculiar matter. I have been arguing that the recruitment of a large number of unprepared black students represented the importation of a weapon that the College would use against itself. Thus, it manifested anti-Oedipal meaning.

But this must be set off against another possibility, which sees the recruitment as maternal, in the sense that the College was offering love to those who needed it, without recognizing that those loved in this way would have their own agenda, with which the maternal could not cope, and who, therefore, came to dominate through their aggression. This would not necessarily be anti-Oedipal, just a legitimate maternal move that had unfortunate results. I will grant that, on the conscious level, there was an element of this. The question is whether there was also an unconscious desire for this aggression.

If the maternal principle had been operating in pristine fashion, I would think that black females, equally unloved, would have been admitted in equal or greater numbers and encouraged to remain. After all, according to the regnant ideology, victimization operated through sex as well as race. Black females would have been twice oppressed, and, therefore, entitled to more compensation, in the form of admission. That the vast majority were men strikes me as indicating that their specifically male characteristics were part of their appeal. It adds another dimension to this already complex picture, and an interesting one at that.

Yalman and Wilson continue:

> Commenting on the sex ratio, Graham notes in her three-year and five-year reports on the APIE how marked the differences were between ghetto males and regularly admitted white male students. Black ghetto males found the white male students precious—perhaps effete and perhaps effeminate. Other respondents have noted ... the sly satisfaction taken by black males in the fear and compliance that could so easily be generated in white students.

> This is something commonly observed in studies in clinical psychology, the aggressiveness of the slum child in the father-absent, mother dependent family. Years ago in a study of dramatic, sometimes violent rites of initiating youth to manly roles, Whiting, Kluckhohn and Anthony (1958, pp. 359–370) found that such rites were linked with protracted male child–mother association and dependency. Then they ask, where, in U.S. society, does one find

similar, virtually ritualized violence among adolescent males? The answer they suggest is that we find such violent conduct in urban slums, and especially in father-absent, mother dominant families—situations in which juveniles, with their gangs and rumbles, their rebellious defiance of authority, their anxious demonstration of virility learn to employ and esteem aggression.

We suggest, then, that the admission in large numbers of very poor ghetto blacks was an unfortunate decision—if, indeed, it was a conscious act. For it added to ghetto-bred aggression the swaggering, muscle-stretching macho of males disproportionately lacking adult male role models. There is no question that providing a fruitful education for black students at Antioch would have had more prospects of success, had the sex ratio been reversed, 70% of the admissions being women. [Yalman and Wilson, pp. 445–446]

It only needs to be added that, from a psychoanalytic perspective, the decision was much more interesting and significant if it was an unconscious act.

But, of course, imputing unconscious motivation is a risky business, fraught with all kinds of difficult and generally irresolvable questions about the nature of argument and proof. To assert propositions about unconscious motivation is to run the risk of being accused of "wild analysis". I do not want to run that risk, even if only because it would detract from the logic, however incomplete, of what I want to suggest. So, I will avoid it by not asserting propositions. I will simply offer a conjecture. I like to think of it as playing a game. The name of the game is sex.

Sex

Freud has been endlessly criticized for saying that everything is about sex. But let us suppose, for the sake of our game, that everything is about sex.

This is necessarily a psychoanalytic game, because psychoanalysis is the only discipline that is configured to make sense of this otherwise outrageous proposition. That is because it uniquely understands that meaning ranges, as I have said, along a dimension of abstraction, without getting lost in the process. When Freud talks about sex, he is talking about intercourse, and he is also talking about "immortal Eros", which Empedocles named as one of the two fundamental principles of the universe. Psychoanalysis understands the unity here.

So it is: a man's penis stands up in an erection and a man stands up and asserts himself. This similarity is not just an artefact of language. Undermine a man's confidence in himself to the point where he cannot assert himself, and look at his penis.

The framework of objectification, the paternal function, is man's representation of himself, and also his claim to have something that the woman will value. On one level of abstraction, this is a matter of the achievement that represents his claim to fusion with a loving world; on another level, it is his penis. But the penis is the biological root of it all, and in some sense we are, at root, animals. It is not a metaphor for anything, but it is that to which metaphors point (Verhaeghe, 1999). Every other self-representation that a man can make can be redefined through self-consciousness. But physical impotence cannot be undone by thought.

Undermine a man's sexual potency and you undermine him. He has been castrated and he cannot stand up.

What were the black students, beginning with the APIE cohort, brought to Antioch for? They were not brought in to be students, in the usual sense. They were not selected for their proven aptitude as students; on the contrary, as we have seen, they were recruited because they would not fit into the established framework. They were there to change the framework, not be students in it. They were brought there to simply be their own unmediated selves; the college would reconfigure itself around them.

Looking back at the selection criteria, we can see that most of these are qualities of dominance; they were called in to be dominant. And now let us go back to our favourite psychoanalytic premise, that it is all about sex. Let us suppose that these guys were called in to be, with apologies for a certain indelicacy of expression, what are best called "studs".

So, was that what it was? Was it that the Antioch women wanted to have sex with these black guys, who did it so much better than the white guys? Or, at least, were collectively imagined to do it better?

The answer here must be no and yes, depending on the group of women in question. In the case of the women who were specifically in the van of the strike, and, indeed, its most violent element, the answer is probably no. Anecdotal evidence in the form of recollections by alumni suggests that these women were generally lesbian. Along these lines, Marge Nelson, the faculty member we have quoted in support of the strike, was quoted in an earlier article to the effect that, "When I came here last summer, I was horrified when women talked about their experiences here. The idea of women as sexual objects is still strong, and women are seen as open and available" (unsigned, 1972).

It is unlikely that she was sexually interested in the black students.

On the other hand, some certainly were. Consider a vignette from Michael Goldfarb, now a writer for the conservative *Weekly Standard* and formerly a National Public Radio correspondent, who matriculated in 1971.

> Within my first week I twice had guns drawn on me, once in fun and once in a state of drunken for real by a couple of ex-cons whom one of my classmates, in the interest of breaking down class barriers, had invited to live with her. [Goldfarb, 2007]

The sexual interest here was clear enough.

But if we simply say that among some women there was sexual desire and among others there was not, we miss an underlying unity here. It is that both lesbianism, as a rejection of male sexuality, and the abandonment of white men as sexual partners in favour of black men, involve the repudiation of the sexual dimension of the white men whom these white women would associate with the father. In this unity, and here I must repeat that I can offer only a conjecture, there is psychological action with very heavy weight.

It suggests that even when the answer was yes, this is what the importation of the black men was all about, there was something deeper than sex going on. The reality was far less important than the fantasies that were in play. My conjecture is that there was a deeper message being sent to the white guys about their standing as men; sex was serving a symbolic function here. The issue was not so much about sex itself, although sex was the fulcrum; it was about the politics of sex.

My hypothesis is that there was a message here about the meaning of masculinity: "None of this paternal function and objective self-consciousness stuff, no logic and mathematics, no wrought achievement in an impersonal world, no literary work that stands out over time. Let's cut to the chase: f—k me right. That is what it means to be a man; and on those grounds, you are a failure and you always will be."

Let us suppose, to continue our game, that the effect, and my conjecture is that there was an unconscious desire here, was to undermine the men's confidence in their sexual offering. That would explain, and I know of no other explanation that even comes close, why their confidence in the more refracted aspects of that offering was lost. Masculinity had been redefined in terms of its biological root, and in those terms the white men had been rejected as inadequate.

They had been castrated, and that, in turn, would explain why they could not stand up for the patriarchal function that had hitherto defined the College.

At any rate, if that was the programme, the APIE black students certainly went along with it, as could have been expected. Recall:

Graham notes in her three-year and five-year reports on the APIE how marked the differences were between ghetto males and regularly admitted white male students. Black ghetto males found the white male students precious—perhaps effete and perhaps effeminate. Other respondents have noted . . . the sly satisfaction taken by black males in the fear and compliance that could so easily be generated in white students. [Yalman & Wilson, 1985]

Of course, we could remove this from its specifically sexual context without changing the underlying dynamic of forces, and we would not be surprised that it would become more extreme:

Graham asserts (1967) that black students used swagger and threat quite consciously to play a cat and mouse game with the very apprehensive white students. But the escalating violence went beyond games. Grant asserts (1972, p. 53) that "violence erupted when a black shot at a white student". [ibid., pp. 333–334]

Whether it had a sexual root or not, this pattern of intimidation represented the force that the College acceded to. It appears there were few that could stand in its way, or understood what was going on.

One of them was Kenneth Clark, the distinguished black psychologist whose work was critical in the Brown *vs*. Board of Education decision. In resigning from Antioch's Board of Trustees, Clark wrote to the Chairman of the Board, Theodore Newcomb, saying,

> Antioch, in permitting some of the more hostile Negro students to coerce and intimidate other Negroes and whites by quashing vocal dissent [lacked] the courage necessary to maintain [the] type of academic climate that permits the freedom of inquiry, freedom of thought, and freedom of dissent which are essential to the life of the intellect. [The College is to be indicted for] permitting a group of students to inflict their dogmatism and ideology on other students and the total college community and [for] being silent while some students intimidate, threaten, and in some cases physically assault the Negro students who disagree with them. [*ibid.*, p. 348]

But it was to no avail. According to a 1974 report by Meyers, cited by Yalman and Wilson, Theodore Newcomb, then Chairman of the Board of Trustees responded to Kenneth Clark's allegation of violence and intimidation generated through AASI and Unity House, by saying that "there's no way of knowing that these threats are a consequence of AASI—they could have been much worse without it" (*ibid.*, pp. 332–333).

It has been my contention that we cannot end our explanation simply by acknowledging that Antioch gave way to this coercion. Nor can we stop by acknowledging that Antioch brought these coercive forces into itself, because we also know that this was no accident; it was done, if not consciously, then at least deliberately. I have been trying to make sense of why it did that.

My hypothesis is that, ultimately, it was about the politics of sex. In the end, the issue was who would be boss. And in my hypothesis that was resolved. She would be boss.

That this was so, that the matter was about sex and the politics of sex, is reinforced by two facts. In the first place, we may note that after the 1973 revolution, the New Directions programme quietly disappeared. What was supposed to be the thrust, so to speak, of the new Antioch, and for which the same arguments could have been made as were made before, was now understood to be inessential. It was not as if the politics of Antioch were changed;

they were more radical than before. However, having served the purpose of shifting power, and showing who was boss, the studs were told, by the new boss, that they were no longer necessary.

The second point relates to the fact that, as we saw at the beginning, the mother as boss can offer no direction. She is, after all, the object of desire. How can she maintain her leadership if there is nowhere for her to lead.

The answer is political correctness, and with it the attack on the father. He could still provide a sense of direction, only in negative form. Attacking him, undermining and destroying his image and significance, would do nicely enough. And here again, this shows up in the politics of sex.

Many who know nothing else about Antioch will know it as the scene of a unique sexual relations policy. In this arrangement, couples engaging in sexual connection needed to specifically ask for and receive permission from their partner at each stage of the progression toward intercourse.

The sexual policy came up in the context of Internet discussions about the way the general public thought about the college. It appeared that the students supported the policy and felt very much abused by the fact that the outside world thought it weird. According to the students, outsiders did not know what the policy was about, which turned out to be the issue of date rape. The meaning of the policy was that it guarded against the possibility of one student taking advantage of the other and, hence, according to the controlling norms, committing rape.

Allen put it this way:

> The extremists in this case consisted of a group of student feminists who called themselves "Womyn of Antioch" . . . and claimed to be reacting to two incidents of date rape on the Yellow Springs campus in 1991, which they said the administration had ignored. No Antioch students were ever charged with those offences either formally or informally, much less found by a college tribunal to have committed them, much less prosecuted for any crime by outside authorities. Antioch's archivist Sanders said that the alleged rapes might have been more a matter of "perception" than reality. None the less, when the Womyn "stormed" (the word comes from Antioch's website) an Antioch community meeting and insisted on pushing through the policy they had drafted regardless

of parliamentary niceties, the administrators and faculty who were supposed to be on at least an equal footing with the students at those meetings, if not their superiors on the basis of maturity and experience, said, oh, okay.

The Womyn-drafted sexual-offense policy read: "Verbal consent should be obtained with each new level of physical and/or sexual contact/conduct in any given interaction, regardless of who initiates it. Asking 'Do you want to have sex with me?' is not enough. The request for consent must be specific to each act." The penalty for even being accused of failing to obtain consent for one of the "levels" was immediate expulsion without a hearing or any other rights ... [2007]

After much public mockery, and some legal threat, the policy was moderated, but still it remains in force. What holds it there?

Getting a handle on this first requires the recognition that Antioch's student body has been, for some time, a majority of women, although in this it does not differ from many others. A more interesting possibility arises from the Internet discussions among alumni. It is that the males were predominately homosexual, and that the straight, white male students felt themselves to be a beleaguered, and even persecuted, minority.

One alumnus said,

Once again, I would just like to throw out there that [name] himself said it was the "gay underground" that has kept Antioch alive. No, I'm not saying only gay people can go to Antioch. Just saying we need to be mindful of our niche.

And another, commenting on this, said,

Yes, we need to continue to appeal to and make a safe haven for, left wing, gay, trans- and cross-gender people, "Queers" (that is their term, not mine!) radicals, etc., etc.

But

During my frequent student interviews over the last 4 years, I was occasionally taken aside by straight white males who told me in whispers with some fear of being overheard that they did feel ostracized and as members of an unwelcome minority. And I have heard of at least a couple of cases where such kids transferred out for that reason.

Allen points out that straight, white males were the only group on campus that did not have an officially recognized organization. For our purposes, the point is that sex, which was celebrated at Antioch to the point of being the core of just about everyone's identity, was paradigmatically homosexual. This gives a rather different slant to Antioch's sexual policy.

If we may assume that the policy arose among white women out of a concern over being "date raped" by straight white males, but that the paradigm of their sexuality was lesbian, this means that the sexual policy has two aspects to it. One is that it would capitalize nicely on the erotic possibilities of restraint. The other is that the unconscious substratum remains, and the sexual transaction has a symbolic content. It is an act of domination over the straight white male, the father. She is saying, "I'm the boss." And, within the drama, the guy acknowledges, "Yes, you're the boss."

But, as we have seen, there is a dialectical dimension to this. In order for her to be the boss, she has to have him to be boss over; she is dependent on him for her own identity. So it goes in the anti-Oedipal.

End of the game of sex: the death instinct

The game of sex is over, but not our investigation quite yet.

As before with blacks, the implication here seems to be that it was women that brought an end to Antioch, and that implication is also off the mark.

My hypothesis is that the active political forces in this process have been women, but, going back to the original premise, I would say they only represent forces that are deeper than political. At that level, the actors are not women. The truth is, they are not even actors. The real issues here are intrapsychic. We externalize them, we even form our ideas of ourselves in that way, and then they can take political form, which is what we have seen here. Then various actors play their roles, thinking that they are the agents in this play. But that they think so is as much a part of the play as their gestures, their words, and their exclamation points.

Ultimately, the energy that underlies the conflict between the Oedipal and the anti-Oedipal is the tension between spontaneity and self-constraint, the Dionysian and the Apollonian, to use other words, that is part of every psyche. It ends only in death, and it structures all of life

But every tension is unstable; the pressures within it press toward its end. To the extent that it is the tension that structures life, these pressures push towards the end of life. That is what Freud called the death instinct (Verhaeghe, 1999).

Note

1. I would like to thank Antiochiana's archivist, Scott Sanders, for very valuable help.
2. Dixon had said,

> There was also a growing feeling that the college might be exploiting minorities. Offie Wortham, whom I mentioned before, certainly explicated those perceptions. This feeling, predominately on the Yellow Springs campus, was articulated in the view that all of these minority students had been really recruited in order to get financial aid for the institution, and that in a sense they were commodities in that market. [Dixon, 146–147]

CHAPTER FIVE

Organization in the age of hysteria

Author's note

T his chapter uses a somewhat different set of theoretical terms
and concepts from those that have gone before. The two sets
are entirely compatible, but point towards different aspects
of the phenomena that are of interest to us. I considered merging
the two sets, but it seemed to me that the explicit translation would
be tedious and would run the risk of losing the nuances that the
two frames bring with them. Accordingly, I have left things as they
are, except in some instances, leaving such translation as an exercise for the reader. Anyone who has followed me this far will see
the connections.

Introduction

Writing of the difference between classical civilization and the Dark
Ages, historian Thomas Cahill observed,

> The intellectual disciplines of distinction, definition, and dialectic
> that had once been the glory of men like Augustine were

unobtainable by readers of the Dark Ages, whose apprehension of the world was simple and immediate, framed by myth and magic. A man no longer subordinated one thought to another with mathematical precision; instead, he apprehended similarities and balances, types and paradigms, parallels and symbols. It was a world not of thoughts, but of images ... They did not argue, for genuine intellectual disputation was beyond them. They held up pictures for the mind ... By the mid-seventh century, the visible image has assumed far greater reality than the invisible thought. [Cahill, 1996, pp. 204–205]

These patterns of mental activity are familiar to psychoanalytic theory. The mental sphere of the "intellectual disciplines of distinction, definition, and dialectic" lies within the register Lacan called "the symbolic". The symbolic comes to us through internalization of the father, who represents external reality and the order we have made to deal with that reality. The sphere of "similarities and balances, types and paradigms, parallels and symbols" is characteristic of the imaginary. It has its roots in the early state of fusion between infant and mother before reality, represented by the father, intruded upon that intimate connection (Schwartz, 2003; Verhaeghe, 1999).

Optimally, the imaginary and the symbolic coexist with one another in a state of fertile tension, a tension whose specific resolutions give us the capacity to adapt to change through the creation of new form, which the sociologists call the diachronic aspect of society. Yet every tension may be seen as a confrontation of two forces, each of which is trying to dominate the other; and we may identify dynamics in which psychological life is organized by one or the other of these forces' attempts at domination. When psychology is organized by the attempt of the symbolic to control the imaginary, we get what Freud called the "anal character", the obsessive–compulsive personality. This is well known. What is less well known, and which I wish to assert, is that when the imaginary takes upon itself the task of dominating the symbolic, we get the mental configuration known as hysteria.

The question of which of these dynamics predominates is of critical importance to organization. The obsessive–compulsive dynamic is consistent with organization, though organization that gives no place to the imaginary may be lifeless, strained, and destructive of the human spirit. The hysterical dynamic, however, is not consistent with organization at all, and, in fact, takes organization as its enemy. If it were to gain too much relative power and become dominant, that could mean the ascent of barbarism.

The age of hysteria

Not too long ago, received wisdom was that hysteria was long gone. For example, Wheelis (1966) maintained that the hysteria that patients presented in Freud's consulting room, in the form of apparent physical maladies with no discernible organic cause, had disappeared from the practice of psychoanalysts. Our times, Wheelis argued, were too psychologically sophisticated to support the kind of repression characteristic of Freud's time. As a result, hysteria, based as it was on repression, has become extinct by becoming impossible.

An alternative view is that hysteria is not only alive and well, but positively thriving, and has simply shifted its symptoms. The shift of symptoms is not some way that hysteria has hidden; it is precisely part of hysteria, and has been since it was given its name and thought to be the result of a moving womb.

This view is suggested, for example, by the work of Showalter (1997), who discusses the rise of widespread social movements that have certain sorts of fantasies at their core and irrationality in the mechanism of their promulgation. The narratives Showalter provides of these movements, which she calls "hystories", support the view, though she does not fully draw this consequence, that hysteria is not a "disease" that exists entirely within the person, as, for example, cancer does, but is a form of relationship between the hysteric and the other.

In this sense, hysteria may be seen as a kind of collusion between the hysteric, usually a woman, and a person functioning as a doctor, or a therapist, or an expert of some sort, who is usually a man. (There are certainly male hysterics. My argument here is that hysteria is based on identification with the early maternal imago. We all have that imago within us and men are capable of this identification, but I suggest that it does not come as naturally to them as it does to women.) The hysteric engages in a performance that is designed to bring a sympathetic response from those around her. On the basis of this performance, the expert diagnoses the malady of the hysteric in terms that reflect social concerns. These terms change over time and circumstance, and, hence, the performance that will create the effect changes; it is geared towards engendering that response. That is one reason that the "symptoms" of hysteria change; one principle of motion of the hysteric's womb.

Showalter finds hysteria in a wide range of contemporary social phenomenal. Some of these, such as the "repressed memory" syndrome and Gulf War syndrome, are close to the classic picture. Others, including the terrible fear about sexual abuse of children in day care centres, and alien abduction, range farther afield. Still, disparate as they appear, these phenomena have a number of things in common.

For one thing, the collusive relationship between the hysteric and the expert never results in permanent "cure" of the hysteric. The symptoms always remain, or recur, though they may change a bit, and are always seen as, in some sense, mysterious. The function of the expert, then, properly speaking, is not to cure the hysteric, but to give a name to her condition. In this way, he legitimates it and makes it, in some sense, real. As such, he is not really an independent expert at all, but, rather, a part of the hysterical drama. I will call him a co-hysteric, and the group consisting of the hysterics and the co-hysterics I will call the "hysterical group".

Second, these are very noisy affairs. There is no suffering in silence among these people. Rather, such suffering is extremely assertive, constituting the basis of a demand that attention be paid to it.

Third, there is nothing outside of these dramas. They are taken by the hysterics to be the whole world, reducing everything else to triviality. The demand they make is, therefore, categorical and absolute, and is asserted without recognition of feasibility or circumstances or any other limitation that reality might impose.

Fourth, on the basis of this demand, a confrontation always takes place between established forms of understanding and the hysterical group, which claims special knowledge that established authority refuses to credit. In every case, the knowledge of the special group is legitimated on the grounds that the hysterics just know what they know. The claimants, that is to say, demand to be taken seriously in the face of a scepticism that asserts the accepted contemporary criteria of what counts as evidence. They feel abused, outraged, and personally attacked when they are not. Indeed, the institutionalized forms of understanding are seen as partly causing their suffering. The co-hysterics, of course, do take them seriously, which makes them part of the same confrontation.

Finally, the narratives of the hysteric, as adumbrated by the co-hysterics, always involve imagery of a certain kind of penetration. Specifically, we find the narrative of a penetration by an alien substance that is damaging to the hysteric or someone with whom she identifies. This penetration may come in a variety of forms, from children being raped, to penetration by a mysterious organism, to being sexually probed by alien beings. However, it is always present and almost always has an explicitly sexual referent, which is experienced with disgust.

We may recall that this was so right from the beginning of the psychoanalytic study of hysteria, when Freud (1896c) found, or perhaps as a co-hysteric placed, the origin of the symptoms of his patients in sexual molestation by the father.

The one case that may be thought to be at odds here is the hystory of abduction by alien beings from outer space, who are thought to represent a superior form of life. There is penetration in this hystory through the defining narrative of being probed by these aliens, apparently for scientific reasons. This probing is experienced as sexual, but it is embraced and valued, and not seen as molestation. The reason for this difference is that these aliens are, after all, alien and superior. Penetration by them is not seen as debasing the hysteric but as raising her up. This is sex that she will allow, largely because it stands in sharp opposition to, and superiority to, what she can get from the local guys.

Yet rich as her descriptive material is, Showalter takes no clear stand on the causes of hysteria, referring to a variety of theories that posit, among other things, emotional distress, women's powerlessness, the authentic voice of silenced women, and so on. In the end, her argument borrows from the theory of hysteria as a disease, and the hysteric as a sufferer whose condition should elicit sympathy. In this way, she passes over the deeper realization, implicit in her own material, that hysteria is not an underlying condition to which attention must be paid, but rather a drama of an underlying condition engaged in for the purpose of garnering attention. To explore the question of where the need for that attention comes from, and the reason why it leads to the dramatics, we need to go beyond Showalter. Fortunately, we are able to do that.

Verhaeghe's theory of hysteria

Current understanding of hysteria owes much to the work of the French psychoanalyst Jacques Lacan, whose impenetrability bids fair to be considered a hysterical manifestation in its own right. We are fortunate to have the work of a number of his students who have cast his thought in constructive and creative ways, and whose work stands on its own merits. In this connection, I will rely on the work of Paul Verhaeghe (1999).

For Verhaeghe, whose debt to Lacan I will take for granted and will not explore, what is characteristic of the hysteric is a discourse, a form of relatedness to the analyst. At its root, the condition of the hysteric arises from the fact that there is no signifier for the woman. This leaves her as a split subject, stuck in the contradiction between being herself and knowing herself; her life, therefore, bereft of stable meaning. She turns to the therapist, a term we can general-ize to refer to the masculine expert, with the demand that he pro-vide her with meaning, putting him in the position of the "one who is supposed to know". He takes up this challenge and offers her a discourse within which she is supposed to be able to find herself. But all he has offered her is language and it therefore, as she makes manifest, always misses the point. The problem is that his language is always his language. It is always masculine, formed for the purpose of objectivity, and, with regard to her, it never suffices. There is always something left over, which Lacan calls *object a*, which is part of "the real", and which represents her spontaneity. So, his discourse always fails, and she asserts her demand again.

What we can see from this is why the therapist always fails, and why he is not really functioning as a therapist or expert at all. The female subject always remains out of his reach, but, by staying out of his reach, yet bringing him to function in the manner of "he who is supposed to know", she comes to be dominant in the relation-ship. The confrontation between the hysterical group, of which he is a part, and the world of established meaning is, therefore, grounded in the spontaneity of the hysteric, which it can never capture. In a sense, it is a battle for control over who will establish the terms of her meaning, and of how they will be established. Hers is a bid to establish her meaning through this confrontation, defined only by her identification with *object a*, which the language necessarily misses.

What we see here is the refusal of the Oedipus complex that we have called anti-Oedipal, and of the father who represents the common meaning through which the world is organized, but which always leaves her unique and ineffable self out of its account. *Hysteria is her assertion of her unique self as against the common meaning that the father represents.*

This analysis lends itself to further refinement. Hysteria, I have said, is a conflict between one's spontaneity and the shared meaning that makes up the world. But there is the basis for such a conflict in every human being. Why does hysteria seem to be a feminine preserve? How does sex come into this? For Lacan/Verhaeghe, this sexual differentiation arises from the fact that there is no signifier for the woman. But why not? What is there about being a woman that resists signification?

On one level, the idea is absurd. Obviously, there is a signifier for the woman. It is "the woman". How is that not a signifier? But, of course, that is not what Lacan/Verhaeghe have in mind. What they surely mean is that "the woman" is a term that stands for the woman, but it does not signify. It gives meaning to no course of action. It is like a chain of signifiers with only a single link. It goes nowhere.

Now, to be sure, there are plenty of meanings that have been taken to follow from the idea of being a woman. One is a mother, a wife, and so on. The problem with these is that they provide a meaning for the woman only in the context of a relationship with a man, whose meaning has been antecedently, and presumably independently, established. Taken as referring to an independent self, the term "the woman" has no meaning. In other terms that Lacan/Verhaeghe would find useful, there is no desire specific to the idea of the woman that would structure a woman's life. The structure of her life requires the desire of a man. That could drive anyone nuts. Hysteria is just what we call that particular brand of madness.

But why does "the woman" have no meaning, while "the man" does? Why is there no desire specific to the woman, while there is specific to the man? To answer this question, I will turn away from Verhaeghe/Lacan for a while and return to Chasseguet-Smirgel (1986).

For Chasseguet-Smirgel, as we know, the central feature of sex differences arises from different relationships to the maternal imago, the primordial image of mother that we all carry, as the central figure in the psychic life of the child. As we imagine her, she is perfect and will make our own lives perfect. Her love is all we can ever need, and is, indeed, the end of need. What is more, her image is not only a powerful image, it is an image of power. Her very presence will make life perfect for us. Her power, and this is what marks feminine power off from masculine power, inheres in her simply being who she is. She does not have to do anything, but only to be. She is Aristotle's unmoved mover.

To again be merged with her is the ultimate object of all of our desire. By the same token, though, it is also the end of our separate existence. Yet, since her power simply consists in her presence, the withdrawal of that presence means absolute devastation. Therefore, she is the object of our love, but for the same reason she is also an object of terror.

As we have seen, the boy and the girl relate to the primordial mother's power in different ways, though, of course, the difference is not absolute. The little girl can imagine becoming a mother, therefore she does not need to fear the power of the mother to the same extent. The mother's power, in the girl's imagination—and of course this is all taking place within her imagination—is the girl's power.

The boy cannot identify with the mother's power, at least to the same extent, but needs her love. His very neediness makes him absolutely vulnerable to the loss of that love. For that reason, his attitude towards the mother, and therefore his attitude towards women, is marked by total ambivalence.

This ambivalence may be resolved in a number of ways. As we know, in Western culture, the traditional way is through the formation of an agenda, which will, on the one hand, offer fusion with the mother, but, on the other, postpone and detoxify that fusion through the project of doing something that will earn it on grounds that maintain the man's existence. He will make himself worthy of her love. He will do something she desires, and this will provide a reason for her to keep him around, to grant him the ground on which he can comprehend and maintain his own existence.

But what does she desire that will lead her to grant the ground of his independent existence? What, Freud famously asked, does woman want?

This is the question that breaks the matter wide open. It is the key to answering the question of why there is no signifier for "the woman," while there is for "the man".

The answer is that woman wants herself, or, rather, she wants to be the self that she is in her fantasy. What else could she want? In her fantasy, she is perfect in every way. Her very existence is perfection. She cannot want anything beyond herself because she herself is the very satisfaction of desire. She is the very meaning of the satisfaction of desire. She cannot have desire because, as Lacan says, desire requires lack; and she has no lack.

The man has plenty of lack. The desire to satisfy this lack provides the meaning for his agenda. What he lacks is her. She cannot have desire, but for that reason she can be the cause of desire. She wants herself; he will give her herself. She is omnipotent; he will create the conditions in which her omnipotence can be realized. These conditions are what we call home, and it will be the place where their fusion is realized; they will have children.

And all of this will take place within a symbolic framework appropriate to its time. The man will attempt to realize it within the world as it is, as he understands it through language as it is.

But he will always fail. The fantasy of fusion will always elude him. *Object a* will always be left over. Yet, there is nothing for it but for him to try again. In the renewed hope of fusion, he will create new possibilities for thought and for action. In this way he will create the world as it becomes. It is this created world, in so far as she buys into it and accepts the terms he has created, or even as he imagines that she does, within which he grounds the basis of an independent existence.

Out of this grows the chain of signifiers, with her as their end. And the meaning that these signifiers have arises from their position within the chain, the chain which leads from him-without-her to him-with-her. That is why there is a signifier for "the man". It means that a man can find himself within the chain of signifiers.

And it is why there is no signifier for "the woman". She cannot find herself within a chain of signifiers because a chain of signifiers leads to her, and she is already there.

Now, what we can see from this is that the chain of signifiers, in its inevitable failure to reach her, will always be inferior to her. But she needs signifiers because without signifiers there can be no desire, and without desire there can be no directed action, there can be no structure for one's life. One can only be overtaken by the upwelling of feeling and self-referential imagery that constitutes the psychotic dissolution of the self. Quite a problem. What will she do?

Well, traditionally, she has done the only thing she could do. If there cannot be female desire, but only male, she will find her place within male desire. She will define herself in the terms he has created to make sense of his own life. She will be a wife. And in this way, she will bring into herself his desire for fusion with her. She will see herself becoming the mother of his children.

More recently, she has fitted herself into social structures, such as organizations of various sorts, created through male desire and, ultimately, given meaning by it. We can foresee that her place within these structures will always be occasioned by a certain strain, perhaps even an anomaly. This is a matter to which we will return.

Meanwhile, we must pause here to reflect upon how marvellously the traditional arrangement fits things together. Neither man nor woman, though for different reasons, has meaning without each other. Yet, these two hopeless contraptions, taken together, provide meaning for each other and through that have created the world in which we all live. Without that, there would be nothing; take it away and nothing will remain. It is almost as if men and women, like penis and vagina, were made for each other.

She was full and lacked nothing. But lacking nothing, she was nothing. Being full, she was empty. He was nothing and needed her fullness to have the idea of becoming something. His attempts to do so created everything, for the purpose of filling her, as they both needed her to be. The world created in this way was and will remain imperfect, but world it is, and is there for all of us to enjoy.

We have not yet arrived at the discourse of the hysteric. We will get there, but first we must go farther in our reflections on this arrangement.

The woman's desire for the man turns out to be her desire for herself, as mediated by the man. It is based on her recognition of the emptiness implied in her fullness. In the absence of an agenda, she cannot simply be herself because that would simply be psychotic explosion. Yet, she cannot provide signification for herself because the entire signification that is available takes her as its purpose. It is all directed toward her pursuit and always contains the limitations of the man's lack. Yet, how can she be limited at all, since the whole premise of her need is her fullness?

She can resolve this dilemma by using her power as object of desire to influence the man. He may have an answer to who she is, but for the reasons we have just seen, this can never be a really good answer. His signifiers, after all, can only be his signifiers. They can never suffice to tell her who she is, since they will never fit. There will always be something left over, which is precisely her, or, at least, her as they both fantasize her to be—the object of desire in the first place. He must, therefore, renew his pursuit of her, refashioning its terms in the hope of success, and each time trying to refashion those terms to better represent her. In this way, she gains meaning by being the object of his attempt to make meaning, ever renewed through the relationship of this pair and the tension between them. End that tension and they both disappear.

So it is that we understand what the tension is all about. It is a contestation about the source of meaning. His meaning is the masculine meaning of the symbolic, which ultimately gains its meaning from its attempt to encompass her perfection, which it can never accomplish. Her meaning is derived from her identification with the primordial mother, which validates and even deifies the spontaneity of her imaginary, but which goes nowhere without the symbolic that only he can provide. It is through the conflict of this tension that the imaginary and the symbolic interpenetrate each other and create the relationship without which both of them are nothing.

And so the tension is, and has to be, absolute. There is, as Lacan again puts it, no such thing as sexual rapport. And it is a good thing, too. There can, however, be rapport between human beings, who understand the meaning of this tension and recognize their individual dependence on this tension and, therefore, their mutual dependence on each other. This does not make the tension go away; it simply has its function understood. In effect, what has developed is a relationship between split subjects who know themselves to be split subjects, a form of relationship that we may call *existential*.

But where is the hysteric in all of this? What I have described here is the tension between the sexes. Hysteria may fit into that, but it is not the whole thing. Where do we draw the line between the hysteric and the feminine?

I think we draw it at the point where the meaning of the tension is not yet comprehended, where the dynamic is not yet seen as the eternal game that men and women play with each other, but is seen as being one-sided, as an invasion of the perfect female by the inferior male. We may, therefore, recognize it as a developmental stage, occurring at the point where sexuality is gaining its ascendancy in the female, but where the place of sexuality in adult relationships is not yet understood. It is, therefore, the characteristic dynamic of the teenaged girl, which we knew all along. (Consider, in this regard, Brown and Gilligan's [1992] study of teenaged girls in which the authors are impressed by the girls' revolutionary potential.)

Now, if the place of sexuality within human relationships is not understood, its meaning must be represented with imagery that gains its power from the girl's specific self-reference, both as a sexual being and as a plenum. Inevitably, then, the imagery will be that of penetration or invasion, and specifically sexual penetration by an alien entity that seeks to corrupt and dominate the girl's perfection and self-sufficiency. Her attitude towards it will be disgust and the rage to expel it. There we have hysteria. (Some may call it "borderline," a term that Lacan himself abjures. I will follow his lead, in this analysis, rather than trying to sort out the mass of confused and contradictory theorizing that characterizes this area.)

Hysteria, therefore, represents, on one or another level of abstraction, the attempt to expel the masculine, with all of its desire and all of the symbolic order that it has given rise to, and its place within the relationship between men and women. Within the dynamic of hysteria, the masculine is experienced as a threat to her perfection and self-sufficiency, indeed, to her very existence, by an inferior agency, which seeks to limit her through terms that do not represent her. The attempt to expel, therefore, comes with a feeling of righteousness and the assertion of the absolute self-sufficiency of her spontaneity—in other words, of her imaginary. But consider that the whole framework of the symbolic, of shared meaning, is a product and representation of that masculinity and you can see that we have arrived at what we were trying to show. Hysteria is the motivating force through which the imaginary attempts to subordinate and even destroy the symbolic.

This analysis helps to explain one of the more peculiar, but characteristic, features of the hysteric. It enables us to answer the question of whether the hysteric is lying when she makes charges that are patently untrue. The answer is that she is not lying. She is telling the truth as she sees it, but her idea of the truth is not the one that is characteristic of the symbolic. Truth is not, as it is in the symbolic, a correspondence between a statement and an objective fact. Her whole project, after all, is to deny and undermine the symbolic, and, therefore, to deny the validity of that form of truth.

Her criterion for truth is essentially aesthetic. For her, truth means the vividness of imagery, in this case of the imagery she is using to represent her experience of invasion. This imagery, at the time, is all she is about. There is nothing outside of it. If she says, for example, and sincerely believes, that she was raped by someone, that means that the image of that rape represents, for her, at that time, the experience of being penetrated that is the centre of her psychic life. (Properly speaking, the root of the various images of penetration is an unconscious phantasy, in the same way that the images of the ego ideal represent fusion, which is also an unconscious phantasy. Note here the spelling *p*hantasy, rather than *f*antasy, a usage that points to its underlying, unconscious nature.) That is why another image could serve just as well, in another time, and one should not be surprised to find movement here, for precisely the same reasons that the ancients thought that hysteria represented the movement of the womb.

We shall now turn to consider the way hysteria opposes organization, but before we do that, there is one irony that needs to be mentioned. The hysteric, as we have seen, makes a life of expelling the symbolic, with its inevitably masculine root. But, in truth, she is as much in thrall to the masculine as is any housewife, since the structure of her life is the same as the structure of the male discourse she is trying to expel; it is only its negation. She needs that masculine discourse if her rejection of it is to give her life any structure at all. The difference between her and the housewife is not that she is free of men, but only that she is related to them in a different way: not collaboratively, but parasitically.

Hysteria and organization

To understand the threat that hysteria poses for organization, we may revisit our earlier discussion of Oedipal meaning, adding the recognition that organizational structure is part of the symbolic, the register of shared meaning. As we know, the root of Oedipal meaning is derived from objective self-consciousness, through which one comes to be able to see oneself from outside oneself, a way that represents reality, as the members of one's society define it. This form of self-consciousness, which begins when one comes to see oneself from the point of view of the father, is not objective in the sense that one sees oneself as one really is, but in the sense that one sees oneself as an object, as others would see you who have no sub-jective interest in you. Its terms represent the social conventions that have been negotiated as a basis of exchange. It is a way for members of the society to pursue their interests in a way that others can understand and which can serve as a pattern of exchange. According to our usage, when a node of this pattern of exchange acquires a certain stability, and when individuals come to rely on it and depend on it, and when they give it an identity and take steps to preserve it, it can be said to be an organization, and the agreed upon patterns can be said to be the organization's structure.

Organizational structure may be considered the synchronic aspect of organization—the specification at any given time of what behaviour is expected of participants as part of their jobs and of how these individual behaviours co-ordinate with each other. The fact that these structural elements are within the symbolic means that we can step outside of them and consider their advantages and disadvantages with some objectivity. In and of themselves, they are not important to us. This makes it possible to design an organiza-tion so that it can attain a goal in the most efficient way. This is, of course, the great advantage of the bureaucratic form of organiza-tion, an advantage that carries forward into their more organic successors—a transformation that can be thought of as representing only the rapidity with which bureaucratic design is reformulated. This is not to say that the imaginary has no place in organization. On the contrary, it represents the principle according to which organizations move through time, both on the level of individual desire and on the collective level of refining organizational structure to pursue a collective goal. In either case, it contains the ego ideal, the motivational substrate that makes organizational behaviour meaningful to participants and breathes life into what would otherwise be ritualized behaviour. But an organization from which the imaginary has excluded the symbolic is impossible. It can exist, so to speak, only in the imaginary, only as a fantasy. The attempt to get there would have to mean destroying organization in so far as it exists, and can possibly exist. Ultimately, that is the danger that hysteria poses to organization.

The antagonism between hysteria and organization plays out through four phases, each of them representing the increased power and danger of hysteria. I will refer to these as *individual hysteria*, *organized hysteria*, *co-optional hysteria*, and *internalized hysteria*. In what follows, I will discuss each of them.

Individual hysteria

As was intimated before, what we can see from this is that the organization must be the site of a permanent confrontation between its behavioural expectations and the hysteric's experience of herself. She will always experience these demands as other and as alien, having no way to align herself with them in pursuit of an ego ideal. She will experience the organization as constraining her in an intolerable, stupid, and even destructive way. Her allegiance will be limited and she is liable to be seen by others as having a permanent chip on her shoulder, or perhaps being a bit screwy. She will see making personal progress within the organization as a way of removing encumbrances to her being herself. Her orientation to the organization will be marked by an attempt to personalize her relationships with powerful figures, especially men, in this way bringing the organization's symbolic under her dominion and have it revolve around her (see, here, Sulkiewicz's [2004] discussion of the "insulator" type of CEO confidante).

Of particular note with regard to the hysteric's reaction to the organization are those confrontations that come under the form of charges of "sexual harassment". In saying this, I am referring to "hostile climate" sexual harassment, and mean to clearly exempt the sort of sexual harassment that is generally called "quid pro quo". The latter represents the demand for sexual favours under colour of authority, and should be seen as a form of extortion.

The charge of "hostile climate" sexual harassment is something else entirely. The American Bar Association defines it this way:

> This occurs when an employee is subjected to comments of a sexual nature, offensive sexual materials, or unwelcome physical contact as a regular part of the work environment. Generally speaking, a single isolated incident will not be considered hostile environment harassment unless it is extremely outrageous and egregious conduct. The courts look to see whether the conduct is both serious and frequent. [http://www.abanet.org/publiced/practical/sexualharassment_hostileenvironment.html]

But what the courts will establish as a valid claim is not entirely predictable and is expensive to find out. As a result, as well as for reasons arising from the shared hysteria, organizations tend to follow very conservative approaches in addressing claims of sexual harassment, which has the effect that often simply the claim of having been sexually harassed invokes the presumption of guilt.

This, obviously, is a situation tailor-made for the hysteric, whom we have defined through the fantasy of having been penetrated by masculine meaning, which is to say, by the symbolic. This may easily lead to the experience of violation even where it has not occurred, either through interpreting innocent or consensual behaviour as invasive, or through the fantasy that such behaviour has occurred. These seem often to mark experiences with figures of authority, which may led us to the hypothesis that it is the penetration by authority itself, as an agency of the symbolic, that is often experienced as a sexual violation. The destructive consequences that can follow from this, in the form of the damage authority itself suffers, and in the wreckage of working relationships that often occurs, are clear enough.

Organized hysteria

The second form of the conflict between hysteria and organization develops when hysteria becomes organized.

The idea of organized hysteria may appear to pose a problem for us. Organization must depend on shared meaning. Yet, if hysteria is a revolt against shared meaning, how can it be organized?

Hysteria can be organized through shared imagery. It represents shared subjectivity, rather than shared objectivity, as organization based on the symbolic represents. It rests on identification and analogy, rather than a common framework of exchange.

Hysteria consists in the experience of being penetrated by masculine meaning, and the attempt to expel it, undermine it, and destroy it. But how that meaning is defined and experienced is susceptible to infinite representation. When hysterics share a representation of that penetration, that forms the beginning of a form of organization. Such organizations proceed through the promulgation and elaboration of the imagery and the social appeal of which it forms the base. That they are not formal, but informal organizations, should not be surprising, given the hysteric's general antipathy towards organizational structure, but their coherence and their cohesiveness should not be in doubt.

An excellent example of this, and one where the experience of masculine penetration is palpable, is Showalter's description of the movement built around supposedly recovered memories of childhood sexual abuse, typically by fathers. This is especially interesting for us, as it takes off from Freud's early theory that hysterical symptoms are the result of sexual abuse, experienced in infancy, of which the memory has been repressed (Freud, 1896c). Freud soon abandoned this theory, but it was resurrected about a century later, beginning with an influential book called *Trama and Recovery* (1992), by a Harvard University Medical School Professor named Judith Lewis Herman.

Herman claimed to have found that "many or even most psychiatric patients are survivors of childhood abuse", which she knew despite the fact that such patients presented with "a bewildering array of symptoms", or "because of difficulties with relationships". Herman said that treating such patients is difficult because "the patient may not have full recall of the traumatic history and may initially deny such a history, even with careful direct questioning" (cited in Showalter, 1997, p. 145).

But such difficulty was far from insurmountable, because the therapist could help the patient, typically a woman, to construct a full narrative, a "memory story". This could then be made public, to therapeutic effect, often by confronting the abuser, who was typically the patient's father (*ibid.*).

What we see here is a paradigm case of the rejection and expulsion of the meaning of the father. In the mind of the accuser, the meaning of the father changed from loving protection to violation and rape. The accusation, which consisted in the verbal performance of this expulsion, was an act of cleansing and recovery. Of course, the meaning of being a father was undermined and lost for the father as well, individually and collectively, as those who lived through this period will well know.

What is of interest for our present purpose is the way this construction became a powerful social movement and determined social events. Showalter quotes an American journalist named Louise Armstrong:

> By the late 1980s . . . the networks had discovered the idea of women's pain and pathology as a daily event . . . By 1993, in the northeast, you could choose from seventeen talk shows between nine in the morning and six in the evening. It was now a rare day when incest was not on the menu.

And she says, "Recovered memory is big business in the United States, with self-help tapes, T-shirts, recovery groups, and even a mass-market best-seller . . . *The Courage to Heal* [which] has sold more than 800,000 copies" (p. 149).

As time went by, organizations, most notably the False Memory Syndrome Foundation, were formed to combat this movement, largely on the basis of evidence of the extent to which a "therapist", with an inclination to do so, could impose distortions on the "recovery" of memories. In the end, they won the day; "recovered memory" has by now been widely discredited. But, for our purposes, it is interesting to note the responses from the partisans of recovered memory to the scientific debunking of their thesis. In this, note the mobilization through and in the name of emotion, and the assault against masculine frameworks of meaning, which are seen as identical with, or at least aiding, the penetrating forces. Thus, Showalter comments on Bass and Davis, the authors of *The Courage to Heal* (1994):

> They remind the reader that debate deters healing and protest that they've been quoted out of context: "Most of the coverage has been extremely adversarial, belittling survivors, depicting them as gullible victims, vengeful children, or simply crazy." Bass and Davis accuse their opponents of being abusers or supporting abusers and charge that pedophiles and rapists stand to benefit from "false memory syndrome." . . . Ultimately, Bass and Davis return to the authenticity of personal feeling: "We must reaffirm that survivors of child sexual abuse are the true experts on their experience. . . . We need to remember that our greatest under-standing comes not in listening to professionals, but to the survivors themselves." [Showalter, 1997, p. 156]

Co-optional hysteria

As I have said, because of the antipathy that the hysteric feels towards organizational structure, organized hysteria tends to be rather informal. It eschews division of labour, hierarchy, and so on. The result is that, while it may be quite powerful, its power is limited to what can be accomplished through the direct application of mobilized emotion, as well as subjected to the instability and lack of focus that always attends emotional force.

A great advance in the potential power of hysteria is accomplished when a hysterical movement gains a formal structure, not by developing one through its own processes, but by gaining control over an existing organization. I call this co-optional hysteria.

A fine example of co-optional hysteria arose recently at Harvard University. The context was an invited address that Harvard President Larry Summers delivered on 5 January 2005 at the National Bureau of Economic Research (available at http://www.president. harvard.edu/speeches/2005/nber.html). In that speech, Summers set himself the task of explaining the relatively low percentage of women "in tenured positions in science and engineering at top universities and research institutions". His argument, which he stated was intended to be provocative, offered three hypotheses concerning this distribution. In his words:

One is what I would call the . . . high-powered job hypothesis. The second is what I would call different availability of aptitude at the high end, and the third is what I would call different socialization and patterns of discrimination in a search. And in my own view, their importance probably ranks in exactly the order that I just described.

His second hypothesis was the one that got him into trouble. He said,

It does appear that on many, many different human attributes—height, weight, propensity for criminality, overall IQ, mathematical ability, scientific ability—there is relatively clear evidence that whatever the difference in means—which can be debated—there is a difference in the standard deviation, and variability of a male and a female population. . . . If one supposes, as I think is reasonable, that if one is talking about physicists at a top twenty-five research university, one is not talking about people who are two standard deviations above the mean. And perhaps it's not even talking about somebody who is three standard deviations above the mean. But it's talking about people who are three and a half, four standard deviations above the mean in the one in 5,000, one in 10,000 class. Even small differences in the standard deviation will translate into very large differences in the available pool substantially out.

Now, Summers moved immediately to distance his feelings about the data from the data themselves. He called it an "unfortunate truth" and said, "I would far prefer to believe something else." And he also said, "I would like nothing better than to be proved wrong . . ." But, as we shall see, these demurrals had no effect on mitigating the storm that followed.

In assessing that storm, one should bear in mind that when he was speaking about the greater variability found among males, Summers was saying something that has been known since Charles Darwin made the observation in *The Descent of Man* (Kleinfeld, 2005). It is one of the best established finding in all of behavioural science (Browne, 2002). It is against the background of this rock-solid finding that the furore against Summers needs to be understood. The point I wish to make is that, from the outset, it was pure organized hysteria.

Let us begin at the beginning, which was the moment that an MIT biologist named Nancy Hopkins walked out of the talk. This is from a 19 January account in the *Washington Post* (Dobbs, 2005):

> "I felt I was going to be sick," said Nancy Hopkins, a biology professor at the Massachusetts Institute of Technology, who listened to part of Summers's speech Friday at a session on the progress of women in academia organized by the National Bureau of Economic Research in Cambridge, Mass. She walked out in what she described as a physical sense of disgust. "My heart was pounding and my breath was shallow," she said. "I was extremely upset." [This is from an article in the *Chicago Tribune*:]

> "When he started talking about innate differences in aptitude between men and women, I just couldn't breathe because this kind of bias makes me physically ill," she said later. [Chapman, 2005]

And again, that if she had not left the room, she would have "either blacked out or thrown up" (Bombadieri, 2005a)

The classic hysterical character of Hopkins' demonstration is clear enough, and commentators soon pointed it out. For example, this is from an article called *Harvard Hysterics*, by the political columnist George F. Will (2005):

> Is this the fruit of feminism? A woman at the peak of the academic pyramid becomes theatrically flurried by an unwelcome idea and, like a Victorian maiden exposed to male coarseness, suffers the vapors and collapses on the drawing room carpet in a heap of crinolines until revived by smelling salts and the offending brute's contrition?

But aside from the dramatics, there were other signs of hysteria that will be familiar to us. Most notably is that Hopkins' response was not directed at the truth of Summers' statements, but at the feelings that they were imagined to represent. And these feelings were rejected in favour of a set of feelings said to be endangered by them. Thus, Hopkins is reported to have said: "It is so upsetting that all these brilliant young women (at Harvard) are being led by a man who views them this way" (Associated Press, 2005). This was despite the fact that, as I noted above, Summers took pains to assert that the data did not represent his feelings.

On the next day, headlines reflected the outrage over his remarks felt by many, first among the attendees, second among the female faculty members at prestigious universities, and third, all over the country, if not all over the world. In general, the criticism focused, as had Hopkins, on the feelings Summers was supposed to have and the unacceptability of the consequences, in terms of the feelings that his feelings were expected to engender.

For example:

> A leading female astrophysicist at Yale, Meg Urry, says she and her female colleagues in science "have talked of little else for days." In the Bay Area, members of the East Bay chapter of the Association for Women in Science "discussed this around the table" at their latest meeting, says their chapter secretary, Paula Shadle.

> "The reaction was frustration, disappointment, and no surprise," said Shadle, a quality assurance consultant to the pharmaceutical industry who has a doctorate in biochemistry from UC San Diego. "One person said, 'Maybe this attitude explains why Harvard hasn't been able to attract women.'" [Davidson, 1995]

In all this, we can see a second index of hysteria. The symbolic has been brushed aside, its existence not recognized. Summers' statements are not acknowledged to have any significance as objective propositions, but only as conveying his feelings, which represent the only reality that needs to be taken into consideration. And the remedy for the low representation of women is also said to be in the realm of feeling. Thus, an essay critical of Summers, written by the presidents of MIT, Stanford, and Princeton, said, "Until women can feel as much at home in math, science, and engineering as men, our nation will be considerably less than the sum of its parts . . . low expectations of women can be as destructive as overt discrimination" (Bombardieri, 2005b).

Interestingly, Summers' remarks appeared to be only the latest in a string of offences which had caused his enemies to feel aggrieved. What were these offences? In a report on a faculty meeting called to hold Summers to account: "Most speakers took aim at Dr. Summers for what they described as an autocratic management style that has stifled the open debate that is at the core of the university's values" (Rimer, 2005).

But an article by law professor Daniel J. Meltzer (2005) offers some insight into what this is about:

Faculty complain that Summers is intimidating, and there is no doubt that he can be. Complaints that he has silenced people, however, need to be rounded out. He seems not yet to have fully found his way in making the transition from faculty member to President, and, alas, the two are not the same; criticism from the President feels different than criticism from a colleague. But that is different from refusing to tolerate dissent. I've crossed swords with him in more than one setting, and while being criticized directly and forcefully by the President can be unnerving, especially in the company of others, one can criticize him back just as directly. That, indeed, is one of his great virtues; he seems to care not about the fact that someone is expressing disagreement but instead about whether the disagreement is persuasive. . . . So while undeniably there is room for improvement in his leadership style, the cries of silencing seem somewhat misleading.

Here, again, Summers' crime was to speak from within the symbolic, with the offence being felt within the imaginary. Having felt penetrated, it moved toward his expulsion. As I write, it has largely succeeded. Summers has kept his position, but the symbolic has not.

From the outset, Summers knew exactly how to grovel:

I deeply regret the impact of my comments and apologize for not having weighed them more carefully . . . I was wrong to have spoken in a way that has resulted in an unintended signal of discouragement to talented girls and women. [Summers, 2005]

But, by itself, grovelling would not do. Summers appointed two committees, packed with his critics, to look into rectifying the situation at Harvard. He accepted their recommendations. Among the concrete results were that Harvard set aside $50 million to address the "gender imbalance", despite the fact that Harvard had already been doing as much as any university to deal with that already, and there was precious little yet to do (MacDonald, 2005). But they had to do something, and what they did was to enshrine the hysterical criticism within the very structure of the university.

This took the form of implementing some of the proposals of the task forces he created. Among them was the establishment along with a number of new deanships, of a new Senior Vice Provost for Faculty Development and Diversity. This new Vice Provost would participate in all faculty appointment and tenure decisions, and would have the responsibility of improving the climate for women and minorities. Among other ways to improve the climate, she would "create a training program to teach professors involved in faculty searches about research indicating that even well-meaning people can harbor hidden biases against women and minorities" (Bombardieri, 2005c).

So, what do we have here?

One does not want to raise alarms without certainty, and pointing to the ways in which institutional arrangements will play out in the future can never be assured of anything more than mild probability. Yet, it is difficult to see these organizational developments as anything but the institutionalization of a system of commissars who would have control over the hiring and promotion of faculty, and, therefore, over the main process through which the university defines itself and specifies appropriate behaviour. The impetus behind this transformation was hysteric, and, therefore, the source of its legitimacy lies in hysteria. Its mission would be to push this hysteria forward. What is more, it represents the authority to overrule policy on the basis of feelings that are presumed to underlie what would otherwise be, at least ideally, rational deliberation. Control over $50 million, by itself, represents a base of power with which to move the institution as one likes.

One could go on, but the point of the matter is fairly simple. Going beyond the limited capacity to organize that is present in hysteria itself, hysteria has gained great influence in an already existing powerful institution that has the full panoply of institutional arrangements necessary to get work done efficiently and reliably and to plan for the future.

Hysteria has co-opted Harvard University, the foremost university in the USA.

Internalized hysteria: hysteria as a philosophy of management

The final phase of the conflict between hysteria and organization comes when hysteria is adopted as a philosophy of management. I call this *internalized hysteria* (I have previously [2002] called this *organizational nihilism*).

Internalized hysteria may begin with a campaign against the organization waged by those who see its processes as penetrating them, or, to use the term commonly employed, oppressing them. Often it is built, as campaigns of the imaginary often are, by anecdotes and stories that relate instances in which the oppressed individuals or groups felt violated. Those who identify with them amplify the force developed here. As of yet, this is nothing but organized hysteria taking place in an organizational context. It becomes internalized hysteria when the management of the organization identifies with them and becomes a part of the hysterical group. We saw this operate above in our discussion of political correctness and organizational self-destruction.

However, internalized hysteria can turn against the organization in an even more basic way, attacking it not for oppressing this or that sub group within the organization, but for oppressing those who belong to the group consisting of the employees of the organization. When that happens, it can take the organization's structure, the organizational necessities that the work requires and imposes, as oppressive, as penetrating the subjectivity. Through this, the organization's energy can be mobilized towards the end of expelling the system's impositions. When that happens, an organization's processes are redirected towards the organization's own destruction, which is to say, the destruction of the organization in its aspect of shared meaning developed through the process of exchange.

We have seen this reconfiguration at Antioch College and it can also be seen at the *New York Times*.

As we know, the younger Arthur Sulzberger, called "Pinch", redefined the role of publisher so that the work of the *Times* was given short shrift in favour of a project whose object was the moral transformation of the *Times* itself, defined in anti-Oedipal terms.

In an early version of the *Times* study, Hirschhorn (2007) suggested that, for Sulzberger, the morality of oppressed *vs.* oppressor is only a part of a broader project of moralization. In this regard, he quotes Ken Auletta (1993):

> He wants more minority positions. He wants more women in executive positions. He wants a less authoritarian newsroom and a

business side that is more nimble. He wants each member of the staff to feel empowered as part of the team. . . . About all his objectives Sulzberger is fervent. In response to complaints about morale or the slow pace of change in the newsroom or on the business side, he has said of his managers with a mixture of determination, cunning and bravado, "I'll outlive the bastards!"

The point is that, evidently, Sulzberger saw this project in which staff were "empowered as part of the team" as part of the same process of moralization in which the oppressed would prevail over the oppressors. Hirschhorn goes on to show that Sulzberger was not just invoking slogans, but put this attitude into action and legitimized it, and that the object under moral assault in this campaign was the *Times'* own authority structure.

Thus, recall the retreat and the town-hall meeting described above, in which Sulzberger essentially authorized attacks against the executive editor and the managing editor, respectively. Bear in mind that Sulzberger is the publisher of *The Times* and hence the top of its management hierarchy. His actions in these settings cannot help but be seen as managerial leadership, from which it follows that Sulzberger had made subordination into a principle of management.

In analysing the causes of this transformation, Hirschhorn notes the culture of "personalism" [which] elevates the salience of feelings in institutional life. This trend is rooted in the currents of a postmodern culture with its emphasis on subjectivity and psychic depth. And also:

> long standing currents in Western thinking associated with utopian thought and strivings— the idea that social life can be constituted so that conflict can be eliminated; that people can live in the social world without experiencing any alienation, any distance between what they wish to experience and express and what opportunities others afford them. [Hirschhorn, 2006, p. 7]

Taking these together, we can see the elevation of the imaginary as a principle of organization. With personalism, we see the apotheosis of individual spontaneity. With the utopian element, we see the guarantee that individual spontaneity may be safely followed, and, therefore, that objective self-consciousness is not necessary.

Psychoanalytic thought leads us to see that the omnipotent, benevolent mother must be the source of that guarantee. What it suggests is that the image of the group implicit in this model, the "empowered team", in Sulzberger's terms, is indeed a group: it is a fusion of infant and child, together with their associated identifications.

Taking this as a model for organization would certainly lead to the idea that the demands of exchange, demands based on a negotiated shared meaning which, by definition, is not our own, would be seen as an imposition, a violation, and a penetration. This draws the linkage with hysteria that we have come to recognize and leads us to appreciate the threat it poses to organization.

Conclusion

The descent of Europe into the Dark Ages was not occasioned merely by the onslaught of Germanic tribes. By the time the barbarians sacked Rome, Roman civilization was already hollow and its army was itself composed of Germanic tribes. In the long descent from its height, it had lost something vital. What was that? Edward Gibbon (1909), speaking of the *Pax Romana*, put the matter this way:

> The vast extent of the Roman empire was governed by absolute power, under the guidance of virtue and wisdom. The armies were restrained by the firm but gentle hand of four successive emperors, whose characters and authority commanded involuntary respect. The forms of the civil administration were carefully preserved by Nerva, Trajan, Hadrian, and the Antonines, who delighted in the image of liberty, and were pleased with considering themselves as the accountable ministers of the laws. [Volume 1, p. 70]

The great emperors of Rome governed under a sense of fealty to, and indeed subordination to, the laws and institutions, the symbolic, of Rome. They saw themselves, and were seen by others, as agents who expressed the authority of shared meaning. The deconstruction of shared meaning, which is now such a prominent part of our political process, is a matter that should concern all of us.

CHAPTER SIX

L'imagination au pouvoir: Britain in the age of Princess Diana

M y purpose in this book has been to show how political correctness, anti-Oedipal psychology, and hysteria attack organizations. However, the highest level of organization does not take the form of specific organizations, but is society as a whole. I have tried to avoid looking at that level of analysis, because it is difficult to identify concrete processes. With that as a caveat, though, I would like to end with a look at the effects of these dynamics at the level of society through the lens afforded by a marvellous film by David Frears, called *The Queen*.

In this film, great pressure is placed on Queen Elizabeth II by the British public to share their grief over the death of Princess Diana. For example, tabloid headlines say, "Show us there's a heart in the House of Windsor", and "Show us you care".

This seems absurd to Elizabeth, who thinks of grief as a private emotion that one should, as with all emotions, keep to oneself. In this, she sees herself as representing British tradition, patriarchal and mildly obsessive–compulsive, which it is her function as a British monarch to uphold. Her belief was that her people would, at any moment, reject that sentimentality, which had been stirred up by the press. They would return to the sober restraint that had traditionally been their manner of mourning, and which the world had always admired.

But the mood did not shift; it got worse. Polls taken indicated that 70% of the public believed that Elizabeth had damaged the monarchy, and that one in four were in favor of abolishing it all together. Elizabeth came to feel herself at odds with what the country had become. There had been a shift in values, and when a monarch no longer understood her people, it was perhaps time to hand it over to the new generation.

But her mother was having none of that. She reminded Elizabeth of the lifelong vow she had taken, which she said was a commitment to God, as well as to her people.

But what if, Elizabeth asked, her actions were damaging the Crown? Her mother thought the idea was absurd:

> Damaging it? You're the greatest asset this institution has; one of the greatest. it has ever had . . . You must show more strength; reassert your authority. You sit on the most powerful throne in Europe, head of an unbroken line that goes back more than a thousand years. Do you think any of your predecessors would have dropped everything and gone up to London 'cause a bunch of hysterics carrying candles needed help with their grief? Ha!

In the end, in the face of clear detestation on the part of the public, who in the crowd scenes that picture them seem to be mostly women, she backed down and delivered a speech that, while not exactly alive with feeling, had enough to bring her back into favour. In fact, Blair told her later that through this act she had become more respected than ever.

What she had said was, in part, "What I say to you now, as your Queen, and as a grandmother, I say from my heart."

Near the end, Elizabeth returned to the idea of transformation, expressing again her belief that the world had changed:

> Nowadays people want glamour and tears, the grand performance, and I'm not very good at that. I never have been. I prefer to keep my feelings to myself. And foolishly I believed that was what people wanted from their Queen—not to make a fuss, or wear one's heart on one's sleeve. Duty first, self second. That's how I was brought up. That's all I've ever known.

Change it had; it had become transmogrified to fit the Age of Hysteria.

It does not go too far to say that the British people did not merely want to mourn Diana; they wanted her symbolically recognized as Queen. They wanted her death to be marked by flying a flag at half-mast over Buckingham Palace, a flag that was historically only a royal standard, indicating that the monarch was there. And they wanted her funeral to be a state affair.

Yet what State would it have been? The structure of the state funeral that was chosen because of its appeal was adapted from the funeral planned for the Queen Mother, except that, in the place of heads of state and 400 soldiers, there would be actors, fashion designers, representatives of various charities, and other celebrities. One can think of no better symbol for the role of the imaginary in the reconstituted Britain.

The point is that Diana's symbolic elevation as Queen did not simply represent the elevation of a person. It meant a shift in what it meant to be Queen, representing a shift in the nature of the society she was supposed to represent.

It appears that such coronation would have been fine with Diana, as her wistfulness in an interview showed, but she understood that it represented a change in the nature of the monarchy.

An interviewer asked her whether she thought she would ever be Queen. She said she did not:

> I'd like to be a queen of people's heart, but I don't see myself being Queen of this country. I don't think many people will want me to be Queen. When I say "many people", I mean the Establishment I married into. 'Cause they decided I'm an outsider. They see me as a threat of some kind. I don't go by a rule book because I live from the heart, not the head.

But any rule book would stand in opposition to living "from the heart". That is what a rule book is. In defining herself in terms of her heart, and defining her heart in its opposition to social rules, Diana fitted herself perfectly into the anti-Oedipal, hysteric frame. And it is clear that the British people saw her and loved her this way, and that this was the basis of her appeal: a talking head being interviewed on television said, "Di was wonderful because she stood up to the Establishment. We have no one doing that now. She said you're detached, elitist people we are paying millions of pounds to be better than us."

To repeat the main point here, by symbolically elevating Diana to monarchy, the British public were redefining the society as that which she would represent. Britain would no longer be the stiff-upper-lip, patriarchal Britain of its past. On the surface it would be the maternal heart-on-one's-sleeve Britain. But our understanding of anti-Oedipal and hysterical dynamics suggests that more would have been involved, for Diana's heart was not just a heart, it was a heart that was defined by its opposition to the traditional order of Britain, perhaps even to order as such.

In calling for the Queen to show her grief over the death of Diana, the British people were, in effect, calling upon her, through their own hysteria, to abandon what Britain had been and accept her subordination to Diana and the hysteria she represented. In demanding the elevation of Diana, therefore, Britain was defining itself against itself.

There is very little recognition shown on the part of the British public that there is anything problematic about this. The single exception is Tony Blair, who registers concern over the fact that the monarch accepting her subordination to the people's will effectively turns the country into a republic, which he said was unimaginable, "because no one would wear it; no one wants it." In our terms, it was not the Oedipal internalization of their own collectively determined order that the British had accomplished, but a rejection of such self-imposition. It was not a taking of responsibility, but a denial of responsibility.

Who will rule? The imaginary will rule. And whose imaginary? There's the rub. Recall that, in all this, Elizabeth was not being asked to express the emotions she had, but rather the emotions she was supposed to have. The fact that she famously did not like Diana was not supposed to enter into this at all. The public was not demanding that Elizabeth wear her own heart on her sleeve, but rather that she wear *their* heart on her sleeve, and that is a different matter entirely. As George Orwell said about the England of 1984, "A Party member is required to have not only the right opinions, but the right instincts." Nothing good can come from such totalitarianism.

Cherie Blair, trying to get a handle on Tony's evident appreciation for the Queen, suggested a possibility that made sense to her; that it was, for him, a matter of the way he related to his mother, who, if she were alive, would be the same age: "You understand how stoical she was: old fashioned, uncomplaining, lived through the War. Oh come on, who does that sound like?"

But Ms Blair gets it wrong on at least two levels. To begin with, obviously, the virtues she described were the traditional British virtues, and more patriarchal than matriarchal. More interesting though, is a point that she massively has missed. Elizabeth, then Princess Elizabeth, not only lived through the war, she, and indeed Tony Blair's mother, for the same reasons, helped to win it.

With the other members of the Royal Family, Elizabeth stayed in London during the blitz. Quietly accepting the danger of being bombed, she served as an example of the courage that the British have traditionally had, and through which they have defined themselves. In this way, she helped the rest of the British people accept danger without submitting to Hitler. As a Princess working as a mechanic, she showed the commitment to the war effort that other Britons would have had to show if they were going to prevail; and they did show it, and they did prevail. Whether a Diana, opposite to Elizabeth in every relevant respect, and the British people who had chosen to be represented in her way, could have won the war is very much in doubt.

The more important question, however, is whether the Britain of Diana, and the West in general, will be able to win the war we are in now. Anyone who has followed my argument will recognize that the odds of this are not very good.

The problem is very simple. They are against us and we are against ourselves.

Conclusion

Political correctness redefines the world, but it does so in a way that living in the world becomes impossible.

This is a matter of ontology. The objective world that the father represents is a world whose most basic processes are morally neutral. Understanding the world means understanding the relationships between causes and effects. These give us the fundamental objective facts which we need to take into account, whose defining characteristic is that they are indifferent to whether we approve of them or not.

The objective framework does not revolve around any of us, and, therefore, is available to all of us. Agreeing on the objective view makes us comprehensible and predictable to one another, which makes it possible to co-ordinate our efforts and co-operate with each other. This gives us each a stake in its maintenance and provides the basis for its legitimation. Within it, we can develop and negotiate moral codes and laws to which we can subordinate our behaviour, knowing that others will as well. Through this mutual subordination, social order becomes possible. Social order is the greatest achievement of Oedipal psychology.

But anti-Oedipal psychology, political correctness, does not accept this subordination. For anti-Oedipal psychology, the fundamental facts of the universe are moral realities; specifically, axiomatic classifications of who is good and who is bad. This does not imply that good people cannot do bad things, or that bad people cannot do good things. It simply means that if good people do bad things, it is because they have been made to do so by bad people, and vice versa, of course.

What gives this vision its terrible hard edge is that, for each of us, goodness begins with ourselves and those with whom we identify, and it extends to the fantasy mother that we all carry with us and whose goodness represents the world's proper and natural response to us. Anything besides love must be a manifestation of badness.

As I have argued, this puts the father, who represents social order, in a terrible position. It turns him into the personification of evil.

This, then, is the way the ontology of anti-Oedipal psychology plays out: we, who are good, are always stifled and oppressed by the bad father. We are properly and morally arrayed against him; we need to destroy social order. By this action we will bring back the world of perfect goodness of which we have been deprived.

More than simply a fantasy, this is a fantasy of fantasy realizing itself. That it is portrayed as morally superior to the order that the father represents gives us an idea of the depths of the quandary we are in, because it is sealed off. By definition, it does not take the indifference of reality into account, and puffs itself up in righteous indignation in its refusal to do so. It demands that fantasy prevail against reality.

We must draw from this the conclusion that political correctness, and the anti-Oedipal psychology that underlies it, is nihilistic.

In *New Introductory Lectures on Psychoanalysis*, Freud discusses the nihilism of the anarchist, *Weltanschauung* (I am grateful to Stephen Rolfe for bringing this to my attention):

> The first of these *Weltanschauungen* is as it were a counterpart to political anarchism, and is perhaps a derivative of it. There have certainly been intellectual nihilists of this kind in the past, but just now the relativity theory of modern physics seems to have gone to

their head. They start out from science, indeed, but they contrive to force it into self-abrogation, into suicide; they set it the task of getting itself out of the way by refuting its own claims. One often has an impression in this connection that this nihilism is only a temporary attitude which is to be retained until this task has been performed. Once science has been disposed of, the space vacated may be filled by some kind of mysticism or, indeed, by the old religious *Weltanschauung*. According to the anarchist theory there is no such thing as truth, no assured knowledge of the external world. What we give out as being scientific truth is only the product of our own needs as they are bound to find utterance under changing external conditions: once again, they are illusion. Fundamentally, we find only what we need and see only what we want to see. We have no other possibility. Since the criterion of truth—correspondence with the external world—is absent, it is entirely a matter of indifference what opinions we adopt. All of them are equally true and equally false. And no one has a right to accuse anyone else of error. [Freud, 1933a, p. 217]

The elements of anti-Oedipal meaning, which one could easily call a *Weltangschauung*, are all here: the elevation of the subjective, the denial of objective reality and the drive to destroy its representations, and even the hint that, if one does so, the fusion of mysticism will be brought about.

Yet, seeing the identity between nihilism and anarchism, on the one hand, and anti-Oedipal politics on the other, exposes a rather revealing contrast between the grandiosity of the politics and the pettiness of its source. The ultimate issue in such politics is the rejection of paternal meaning. But, as I tried to show with the analysis of hysteria, that rejection comes down to this accusation: "Who are you to tell me what to do?"

Does a drive to destroy the whole world come from this motive?

Well, yes, it can come from there, and it does. Indeed, it seems that the triumph of pettiness is what this whole project has been all about. The maternal, after all, loves us exactly as we are; we do not need to do anything, but only to be. The paternal demands more of us. We cannot simply rest content in our organismic identity. Something more is called for. We must become somebody, accomplish something, make something of ourselves.

We require both of these: unconditional love and the demand for achievement. In truth, there is no contradiction between them, but only a division. That is why God, in His wisdom, has given us both mother and father. However, there should be no doubt that demands for accomplishment in the cultural sphere, individually and collectively those things that have made it possible for us to rise above triviality and become significant, have come from the paternal side. The paternal side, by giving us a view of ourselves from outside ourselves, gives us a sense of proportion and makes it possible to differentiate between these two. In this way, it defines significance.

So, when we choose the infantile and cast out the paternal, we destroy not only greatness, but the very idea of greatness. A certain pettiness, which is really only a refraction of the overweening narcissism we have managed to preserve and ensure, is the inevitable result.

We find ourselves drawn, in the present dangerous times, to go beyond the question of whether we, as a species, shall survive. The more difficult question is whether it matters whether we do or not. This is a question that cannot be resolved by analysis, but only by faith.

It remains to be seen whether civilization, in the face of the terrible technological possibilities that it, itself, has created, can find that faith.

REFERENCES

Abramson, H., Casey, L., & Greenfeld, C. (1973). The strike is on. *The Record*, 20 April.

Adams, J. S. (1963). Toward an understanding of inequity. *Journal of Abnormal and Social Psychology*, *67*: 422–436.

Administrator (2006). Buford, architect of UCC's 'Stillspeaking' campaign, to assume new role. News section of UCC website, 7 June.

Allen, C. (2007). Death by political correctness: who killed Antioch College? *Weekly Standard*, 12 November, http://www.weeklystandard. com/Content/Public/Articles/000/000/014/306jqecg.asp.

Amnesty International (2000). USA: a life in the balance: the case of Mumia Abu-Jamal.

Associated Press (2005). Harvard president criticized over comments about women's performance in science, mathematics. *Boston Globe*, 17 January.

Auletta, K. (1993). Opening up the *Times*. *New Yorker*, 28 June, http://www.kenauletta.com/openingupthetimes.html.

Bamber, D., & Bisset, S. (2000). Violent crime rises sharply in rural areas. *The Electronic Telegraph ISSUE*, Sunday 8 October 1962.

Barnard, C. (1951). *The Functions of the Executive*. Cambridge, MA: Harvard University Press.

Barry, D., Barstow, D., Glater, J. D., Liptak, A., & Steinberg, J. (2003). Correcting the record: *Times* reporter who resigned leaves long trail of deception. *New York Times*, 11 May.

Bass, E., & Davis, L. (1994). *The Courage to Heal: A Guide for Women Survivors of Child Sexual Abuse* (3rd edn, revised and expanded). New York: Collins Living, first published 1988.

Bernstein, R. (1991). The rising hegemony of the politically correct. *New York Times*, 28 October 1991, IV 1, 4.

Blair, J. (2004). *Burning Down My Masters' House: My Life at The New York Times*. Beverly Hills, CA: New Millennium Press.

Blau, P. M. (1964). *Exchange and Power in Social Life*. New York: Wiley, 1964.

Bloomberg News (2001). Judge to OK racial-bias deal in Coke case. *Seattle Times*, 30 May.

Boehlert, E. (2003). The forbidden truth about Jayson Blair: it's the issue nobody at the *New York Times* wants to discuss: were a reporter's flagrant journalistic abuses overlooked because he's black? *Salon.com*, 15 May.

Bombardieri, M. (2005a). Summers' remarks on women draw fire. *Boston Globe*, 17 January.

Bombardieri, M. (2005b). 3 university chiefs chide Summers on remarks. *Boston Globe*, 12 February.

Bombardieri, M. (2005c). Harvard improves on tenure offers to women: halts 3-year decline with Summers at helm. *Boston Globe*, 1 August, http://www.boston.com/news/local/articles/2005/08/01/harvard_improves_on_tenure_offers_to_women/.

Boswell, J. (1981). *Christianity, Social Tolerance, and Homosexuality: Gay People in Western Europe from the Beginning of the Christian Era to the Fourteenth Century*. Chicago, IL: University of Chicago Press.

Branch, C. (1994). Re-imagining god, the watchman expositor, *11*(5), http://www.watchman.org/reltop/reimagin.htm.

BRF Witness (1994). Editorial, May/June, *29*(3), http://www.brfwitness.org/Articles/1994v29n3.htm.

Brown, L. M., & Gilligan, C. (1992). *Meeting at the Crossroads: Women's Psychology and Girls' Development*. Cambridge MA: Harvard University Press.

Browne, K. R. (2002). *Biology at Work: Rethinking Sexual Equality*. New Brunswick, NJ: Rutgers University Press.

Buchanan, W. (2006). TV networks reject ad from church—say spot welcoming gays is controversial. *San Francisco Chronicle*, 28 March, p. D-12.

Butterfield, F. (2001). Urban police jobs are losing their appeal. *The New York Times*, 30 July.

Cahill, T. (1996). *How the Irish Saved Civilization*. New York: Anchor.

Cantor, G. (1996). Would policies at the University of Michigan make the perfect test case for affirmative action? *Gannett News Service*, 13 July.

Carlson, S. (2007). A house divided: after years of ignoring financial realities, Antioch College failed while its more-commercial branches survived. *Chronicle of Higher Education*, 29 June, p. A-20.

CEP/Equip (1997). Apostasy in America, March/April, 3(2), www.pcanet.org/cep/Publications/EquipArchives/9703-Apostasy.

Chapman, S. (2005). Staying mute on men vs women differences. *Chicago Tribune*, 23 January, http://articles.chicagotribune.com/2005-01-23/news/0501230329_1_summers-remarks-president-lawrence-summers-positions-at-elite-universities.

Chasseguet-Smirgel, J. (1986). *Sexuality and Mind: The Role of the Father and the Mother in the Psyche*. New York: State University of New York Press.

Christian Century (1994). A converted conference—RE-Imagining, 16 February.

Clarke, K. (1969). *Civilisation: A Personal View*. London: British Broadcasting Corporation.

Clines, F. X. (2001). Police in Cincinnati pull back in wake of riots. *New York Times*, 19 July, http://www.nytimes.com/2001/07/19/national/19CINC.html.

Cohen, P. (2008). The college that would not go gently. *New York Times*, 20 April, www.nytimes.com/2008/04/20/education/edlife/antioch.html.

D'Souza, D. (1995). *The End of Racism*. New York: The Free Press.

Davidson, K. (1995). Harvard president under microscope: female scientists debate comments on gender, science. *San Francisco Chronicle*, 31 January, http://sfgate.com/cgi-bin/article.cgi?file=/c/a/2005/01/31/MNG02B326R1.DTL.

Deogun, N. (1999). Atlanta defends Coke against bias: black employees sue, but support may be slow in coming. *Wall Street Journal*, 4 June, p. 2A.

Dixon, E. (Ed.) (1991). *Antioch: The Dixon Era, 1959–1975: Perspectives of James P. Dixon*. Saco, Maine: Bastille Books.

Dobbs, M. (2005). Harvard chief's comments on women assailed: academics critical of remarks about lack of gender equality. *Washington Post*, 19 January: A02.

Donnelly, F. X. (2001). New mantra: back to basics. *The Detroit News*, 31 October, p. 4A.

Dowling, W. C. (1999–2000). Enemies of promise: why America needs the SAT. *Academic Questions*, 13(1): 6–24.

Edley, C. Jr. (1996). *Not all Black and White*. New York: Hill and Wang.

Eggerton, J. (2004). UCC challenges Miami licenses broadcasting & cable, 9 December, http://www.broadcastingcable.com/article/CA486541.html.

Farber, D. A., & Sherry, S. (1997). *Beyond all Reason: The Radical Assault on Truth in American Law*. New York: Oxford University Press.

Frankel, B. (2000). Coca-Cola commits $1 billion to five-year diversity initiative. *DiversityInc.com*, 16 May.

Freud, S. (1896c). The aetiology of hysteria. *S.E., 3*: 186–221. London: Hogarth.

Freud, S. (1914c). On narcissism: an introduction. *S.E., 14*: 67–102. London: Hogarth.

Freud, S. (1921c). *Group Psychology and the Analysis of the Ego. S.E., 18*: 67–143. London: Hogarth Press.

Freud, S. (1923b). *The Ego and the Id. S.E., 19*: 3–66. London: Hogarth.

Freud, S. (1930a). *Civilization and Its Discontents. S.E., 21*: 59–145. London: Hogarth.

Freud, S. (1933a). *New Introductory Lectures on Psycho-analysis. S.E., 22*: 3–182. London: Hogarth.

Gibbon, E. (1909). *The History of the Decline and Fall of the Roman Empire, Volume 1*, J. B. Bury (Ed.). London: Methuen.

Goldfarb, M. (2007). Where the arts were too liberal. *New York Times*, 17 June, http://www.nytimes.com/2007/06/17/opinion/17goldfarb.html.

Gouldner, A. W. (1960). The norm of reciprocity: a preliminary statement. *American Sociological Review, 25*: 161–178.

Graham, J. (1967). The Antioch program for interracial education—the first three years, 1964–1967. Unpublished reports available at Antiochiana.

Groseclose, T., & Milyo, J. (2005). A measure of media bias. *Quarterly Journal of Economics, 70*(4): 1191–1237.

Gurin, P. (1999). *Expert Report of Patricia Gurin*. Ann Arbor, MI: University of Michigan Press.

Hale, S. (2001). Homicide rate up 27.6% for year in L.A. Violence: central and south areas are the hardest hit. Many of the killers are thought to be gang members. *Los Angeles Times*, 3 January, p. B-1.

Hamilton, M. S., & McKinney, J. (2003). Turning the mainline around: new sociological studies show that evangelicals may well succeed at renewing wayward Protestantism. *Christianity Today*, Week of July 21 07/25/.

Hansen, F. (2003). Diversity's business case doesn't add up. *Workforce*, April, pp. 28–32.

Herman, J. L. (1992). *Trauma and Recovery*. New York: Basic Books.

Hirschhorn, L. (2006). The fall of Howell Raines and *The New York Times*: a study in the moralization of organizational life (working paper), http://www.cfar.com/Documents/Raines.pdf.

Hirschhorn, L. (2007). The fall of Howell Raines and The *New York Times*: a study in the moralization of organizational life. *Consulting Psychology Journal: Practice and Research*, *59*(3): 155–174.

Homans, G. C. (1950). *The Human Group*. New York: Harcourt Brace Jovanovich.

Horowitz, D. (1998). *The Politics of Bad Faith: The Radical Assault on America's Future*. New York: Touchstone.

Horowitz, D. (2001). Progressive crime wave. *FrontPageMagazine.com*, 10 July.

Howard, S. (1973). Union rep urges shutdown tactics. *The Record*, 19 February, p. 1.

Jaschik, S. (2007). Leon Botstein on the "tragedy" of Antioch. *Inside Higher Education*, 2 August, http://www.insidehighered.com/.

Johnson, B. D., Hoge, R., & Luidens, D. A. (1993). Mainline churches: the real reason for decline. *First Things*, 31 March: 13–18.

Johnston, P. (2001). 28pc of robbery arrests are black people, says report. *The Electronic Telegraph*, Issue 2065, 19 January.

Keyes, R. (2007). Present at the demise: Antioch College, 1852–2008. *Chronicle of Higher Education*, *53*(46): B8.

Kleinfeld, J. (2005). Truth to power: Summers of academic discontent. *National Review Online*, 25 January, http://www.nationalreview.com/comment/kleinfeld200501250746.asp.

Klepal, D., & Andrews, C. (2001). Stories of 15 black men killed by police since 1995. *Cincinnati Enquirer*, 15 April.

Klepal, D., & Perry, K. (2006). Cincinnati shrinking, and fast: Queen City falls below Detroit as suburbs gain. *Cincinnati Enquirer*, 21 June, http://news.cincinnati.com/article/20060621/NEWS01/606210361/Cincinnati-shrinking-and-fast

Kochan, T., Bezrukova, K., Ely, R., Jackson, S., Joshi, A., Jehn, K., Leonard, J., Levine, D., & Thomas, D. (2002). *The Effects of Diversity on Business Performance: Report of the Diversity Research Network*. Cambridge, MA: Massachusetts Institute of Technology.

Kneeland, D. E. (1973). Strike catches Antioch in web of its liberal tradition. *New York Times*, 29 May.

Kuran, T. (1995). *Private Truths, Public Lies: The Social Consequences of Preference Falsification*. Cambridge, MA: Harvard University Press.

Kwan, J. L. (2000). "Diversity must be a priority," HP's Fiorina tells execs: tough critique concludes digital divide conference. *San Jose Mercury-News*, 4 May 2000, 1C.

Lacan, J. (1988). Seminar on "The Purloined Letter". In: *The Purloined Poe*. Baltimore, MD: Johns Hopkins University Press.

La Croix, E. (2003). Student strike divided Antioch College campus. *Yellow Springs News*, 20 November.

Lambeth Commission on Communion (2004). *The Windsor Report*. London: Anglican Communion Office.

Lawry, S. (2006). Lawry delivers State of the College. *Antiochian: The Antioch College Alumni Magazine*, Autumn, pp. 5–7.

Lemann, N. (1999). *The Big Test*. New York: Farrar, Strauss, and Giroux.

Leo, J. (2001). Coverage of Cincinnati riots is about attitudes, not facts. *Townhall.com*, 23 April.

Lerner, R., & Nagai, A. K. (2001). A critique of the expert report of Patricia Gurin in Gratz vs Bollinger. Washington, DC: Center for Equal Opportunity, http://www.ceousa.org/pdfs/Gurin1.pdf.

Lewis, M. (2001). *The New New Thing: A Silicon Valley Story*. New York: Penguin.

Lynch, F. (1997). *The Diversity Machine: The Drive to Change the "White Male Workplace"*. New York: Free Press.

MacDonald, H. (2003). What Really Happened in Cincinnati? *Are Cops Racist?* Chicago: Ivan R. Dee.

MacDonald, H. (2005). Harvard's new Old-Girl Network. *City Journal*, 29 July.

March, J. G., & Simon, H. A. (1958). *Organizations*. New York: Wiley.

Margolick, D. (2003). The *Times*'s restoration drama. *Vanity Fair*, August, pp. 143, 196, 199.

Meltzer, D. J. (2005). FOCUS: the complexities of academic leadership. *The Harvard Crimson*, 18 February, http://www.thecrimson.com/article/2005/2/18/focus-the-complexities-of-academic-leadership/.

Meyers, M. (1974). Black education at Antioch College. *Youth and Society*, 5(4): 379–396.

Morgan, A. E. (1929). Almus Pater: Antioch introduces a masculine element into higher education. *Atlantic Monthly*, June, pp. 3–11.

New York Times (2003). Correcting the record: the articles; witnesses and documents unveil deceptions in a reporter's (unsigned compilation), 11 May, p. 1.

O'Connor, S. D. (2003). Opinion in the case of Grutter vs Bollinger et al. Washington, DC: United States Supreme Court.

Orwell, G. (1945). *Animal Farm*. London: Secker & Warburg.

Orwell, G. (1949). *1984*. London: Secker & Warburg.

Osborne, K. (2006). Deadly city: crime report is bleak; Mallory under the gun. *CityBeat*, http://www.citybeat.com/cincinnati/article-1065-news-deadly-city.html.

Pappu, S. (2003). Jayson Blair talks: "So Jayson Blair could live, the journalist had to die". *New York Observer*, 21 May, http://www.observer.com/node/37795.

Raines, H. (2003). Howell Raines discusses the investigation by the *New York Times* into plagiarized and fabricated material by former staff writer Jayson Blair. *All Things Considered*, Interviewer Melissa Block, transcript available from National Public Radio: 8 May.

Ramist, L., Lewis, C., & McCamley-Jenkins, L. (2001). Using achievement tests/SAT II: subject tests to demonstrate achievement and predict college grades: sex, language, ethic, and parental education groups. New York: College Entrance Examination Board.

Ray, J. (2006). Thinly disguised anti-Christian propaganda, 31 March, http://pcwatch.blogspot.com.

Rimer, S. (2005). Professors at Harvard confront its President. *New York Times*, 16 February.

Schwartz, H. S. (1990). *Narcissistic Process and Corporate Decay: The Theory of the Organization Ideal*. New York: New York University Press.

Schwartz, H. S. (2002). Political correctness and organizational nihilism. *Human Relations*, 55(11): 1275–1294.

Schwartz, H. S. (2003). *The Revolt of the Primitive: An Inquiry into the Roots of Political Correctness*. Piscataway, NJ: Transaction.

Showalter, E. (1997). *Hystories: Hysterical Epidemics and Modern Media*. New York: Columbia University Press.

Sidoti, L. (2001). Cincinnati protests, curfew continue. *Washington Post Online*, 14 April, http://Washingtonpost.com.

Sparks, L. (1968). Separatism at Antioch: a study of the Antioch Interracial Education Program. Unpublished reports available at Antiochiana.

Stein, M. (2000). After Eden: envy and the defences against anxiety paradigm. *Human Relations*, 53(2): 193–211.

Sulkiewicz, K. J. (2004). Worse than enemies: the CEO's destructive confidante. *Harvard Business Review*, February, http://hbr.org/2004/02/worse-than-enemies/ar/1

Sulzberger, A. O. Jr. (2006). Commencement address to the graduating class at the State University of New York, New Paltz, http://www.newpaltz.edu/commencement/sulzberger.html.

Summers, L. (2005). Letter from President Summers on women and science, 19 January, http://www.president.harvard.edu/speeches/2005/womensci.html.

Thernstrom, S., & Thernstrom, A. (1999). *America in Black and White: One Nation, Indivisible*. New York: Touchstone.

Tifft, S., & Jones, A. (1999). *The Trust: The Private and Powerful Family Behind The New York Times*, New York: Little, Brown and Company.

Tizon, A., & Forgrave, R. (2001). Wary of racism complaints, police look the other way in black neighborhoods. *Seattle Times*, Tuesday 26 June, http://community.seattletimes.nwsource.com/archive/?date=20010626&slug=police26m

Truby, M. (2000). Diversity gives Ford a new look: aggressive recruiting of minorities and women is sweeping away old guard. *The Detroit News*, 20 August, p. 11A.

Truby, M. (2001a). Age-bias claims jolt Ford culture change. *The Detroit News*, 29 April, p. 1A.

Truby, M. (2001b). Whistleblower takes on Ford: insider offers documents he says prove the company discriminates to achieve diversity. *The Detroit News*, 1 July, p. 1A.

Truby, M. (2001c). Nasser out: chairman Bill Ford assumes CEO post: first Ford to run company in two decades. *The Detroit News*, 30 October, p. 1A.

Truby, M. (2001d). Nasser's demise ends uneasy partnership to remake company. *The Detroit News*, 30 October.

Turner, P. (2003). The Episcopalian preference. *First Things Magazine*, November, pp. 28–33.

Turner, P. (2005). An unworkable theology. *First Things Magazine*, June–July, pp. 10–12.

Unsigned (1972). Women hold open house; discuss sexism at Antioch. *Record*, 14 July, p. 3.

Verhaeghe, P. (1999). *Does the Woman Exist? From Freud's Hysteric to Lacan's Feminine*. New York: Other Press.

Weber, M. (1947). *The Theory of Social and Economic Organization*, Henderson and Parsons (Trans.). Glencoe, IL: Free Press.

Weick, K. E. (1969). *The Social Psychology of Organizing*. Reading, MA: Addison-Wesley.

Wheelis, A. (1966). *Quest for Identity*. New York: Norton.

Will, G. (2007). Farewell, Antioch. http://www.townhall.com/Columnists/GeorgeWill/2007/07/15/farewell,_antioch.

Will, G. F. (2005). Harvard hysterics. *Washington Post*, 27 January: A19.

Wilson, E. K. (1985). What counts in the death or transformation of an organization? *Social Forces*, 64(2): 259–280.

Wood, T. E., & Sherman, M. L. (2001). *Race and Higher Education: Why Justice Powell's Rationale for Racial Preferences in Higher Education Must Be Rejected*. Princeton, NJ: National Association of Scholars.

Yalman, J. O., & Wilson E. K. (undated). *Crisis and Change in an Organization: A Case Study of Antioch College* (draft version). Yellow Springs, OH: Antiochiana Collection, Olive Kettering Library, Antioch University.

INDEX